117.03°

HIDALGO, GUANAJUATO

100.56°

UNION, OHIO

84.30°

UNION, OHIO

84.30°

MEXICO CITY, CIUDAD DE MÉXICO

MONTERREY, NUEVO LEÓN

100.31°

EL PASO, TEXAS

106.48°

TIJUANA, BAJA CALIFORNIA

117.03°

TIJUANA, BAJA CALIFORNIA

117.03°

TWO SIDES OF THE BORDER

REIMAGINING THE REGION

TATIANA BILBAO ESTUDIO

EDITED BY
TATIANA BILBAO, NILE GREENBERG AND AYESHA S. GHOSH

PHOTOGRAPHS BY IWAN BAAN

YALE SCHOOL OF ARCHITECTURE

LARS MÜLLER PUBLISHERS

ESSAYS

PHOTOGRAPHS — IWAN BAAN

MAPS

STUDIO INDEX

PREFACE

DEBORAH BERKE
DEAN, YALE SCHOOL OF ARCHITECTURE

Tatiana Bilbao began teaching at Yale in 2015, inviting us to turn our attention to Mexico. I have always valued her talent as a designer, educator and leading voice in contemporary architecture. She has now presided over three studios that have drawn inspired and provocative work from our students. The latest, held here in the spring of 2018, was also part of an alliance of studios taught in architecture schools across the US and Mexico that used design to address social, political and ecological concerns along the two countries' long-shared border.

I was thrilled when Tatiana brought the idea of hosting an exhibition of the thirteen participating studios in our gallery. Iwan Baan's photographic essay was the perfect complement. These design and documentary projects are not about division, but bridging. They draw together a region with a long history of shared interests that defy current demarcations and hint at a fruitful and interwoven future. In this current political moment, we are honored to support this creative outpouring that colors outside the borderlines.

I would like to express my gratitude to Tatiana for bringing the show to us. I would also like to thank Nile Greenberg for his design and all the contributing schools, both educators and students, who sent their work to us for inclusion. I am grateful to Iwan Baan for logging all those miles and allowing us to see the region through his eyes. At Yale, I would like to thank our director of exhibitions, Andrew Benner, and Alison Walsh, exhibitions coordinator, for working with Tatiana and Nile to realize the show in our space; additional thanks to Luke Bulman, a member of our faculty, for his design of this volume; and to Elise Jaffe + Jeffrey Brown for their support. All of that work — student design, faculty direction, meaningful photography and cartographic research — led in turn to this beautiful book, a lasting document of the effort, insights and aspirations of many creative individuals on both sides of the border and around the world.

FOREWORD: A NEW ATLAS

NILE GREENBERG

Two Sides of the Border is an atlas for a new territory. The academic initiative led by Tatiana Bilbao, Iwan Baan's photographic project, the traveling exhibition and the book all form this new atlas. Within the nations of the US and Mexico lies a region formed by a network of people, commerce, culture, education, labor, food, money, infrastructure and family. By merely participating in the project, all of the practitioners, educators and students are engaged in a shared reimagination of the region, and this book can act as a guide through it.

This book is unlike any atlas you may have viewed, but it embodies the familiar project of trying to draw and describe the indiscernible qualities of a place. The voices in this atlas are from all across the region, San Francisco, Oxkutzcab, Riverhead, Tijuana, Ohio. . . . *Reimagining The Region* is not an examination of the border, but of the shared lives within the region. Alone, you are not able to comprehend or imagine a region. No amount of personal experiences, citizenships, research or a deep interest in the topic will give you the full perspective. When we're imagining something this large we must trust in other stories and perspectives.

When we first began this project we looked closely at the books and essays of Valeria Luiselli. Her work presided over the project as a powerful Mexican-American writer. In one book in particular, *The Story of My Teeth*, she uses a literary technique of layering multiple narratives on top of one another, each illuminating a particular truth. The book tells the story of an auctioneer who auctions each of his teeth off and the incredible encounters each tooth represents. It is in essence an atlas of a story.

The first articulation of this project occurred as an exhibition at the Yale Architecture Gallery in the Fall of 2018. I had taught the initiative alongside Tatiana and she asked me to curate and design the exhibition. From the beginning of the project the importance of things like books was clear to both of us — we chose to design the exhibition like a reading room, a precious place where you might examine a map that was hundreds of years old. In the central space were enormous tables the same size of the iconic Yale piers. With reading lights hovering just above, these students' works were presented as precious objects worth caring about. The tables and walls were each wrapped in a tan fabric, emulating the warm reading room of the nearby Yale Center for British Art. Surrounding these tables were the four cardinal directions, three walls were made from four-foot panels, each one a frame for a glistening metallic Iwan Baan print. In the fourth direction was a double-height wall holding 20 maps from the history of US and Mexico mapmaking. Each panel was designed as if a chapter from a book, and each panel a different page — introductions, plates, appendixes and colophon.

The book that these chapters were forming is our curatorial framework, an atlas in three parts: objective, subjective and projective. The objective atlas is the traditional form, a stack of maps that reflect recent and historical perspective of the border. The subjective atlas is the photography project by Iwan Baan — capturing the changing landscapes, people and architecture of the region in the way that only Iwan Baan can. The projective atlas is capturing the future of the region, 129 student perspectives creating optimistic, dystopian, joyous or devious images of

the region. Together these three chapters in the atlas articulated different truths about what the region looked like.

This is the beauty of the atlas, and if you didn't already understand how this worked, it would appear to be a contradiction. These simultaneous truths are what make any region legible. These compendiums of truths about a region forms an atlas. It is with this definition that we eschew the logic and aims of a "book" and absorb those of an atlas.

In our atlas, in the pages to follow, there are so many voices, each one executing a tiny truth — but together they form the image of a region. The prompt for each professor, student, writer, editor or photographer was to reimagine the region — to consider the region as a shared place rather than two nations abutted against a fractious line. It is sadly true that many people are stranded at the border, held captive by a broken visa system and a shattered justice system, but while those 3,141 km may occupy our political imagination, there is also a rich life straddling that line.

A region is only possible when we're imagining together — redrawing the lines, reconsidering what it means to be a nation and carefully observing our shared history and geography.

TWO
OF THE SIDES
BORDER
YALE SCHOOL OF
ARCHITECTURE GALLERY
11.29.2018 – 2.9.2019

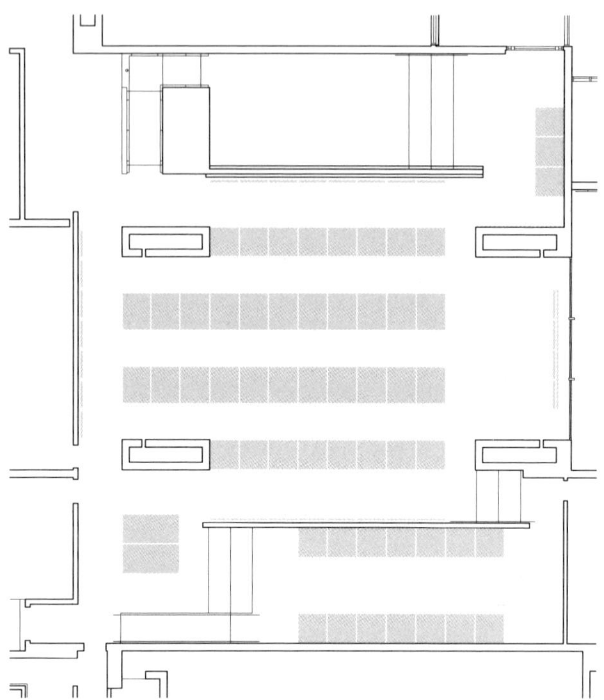

Yale School of Architecture Gallery, New Haven, Connecticut

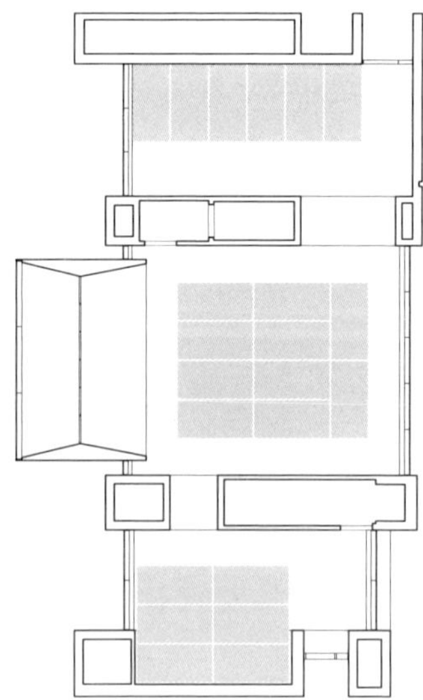

Fay Jones School of Architecture and Design, Fayetteville, Arkansas

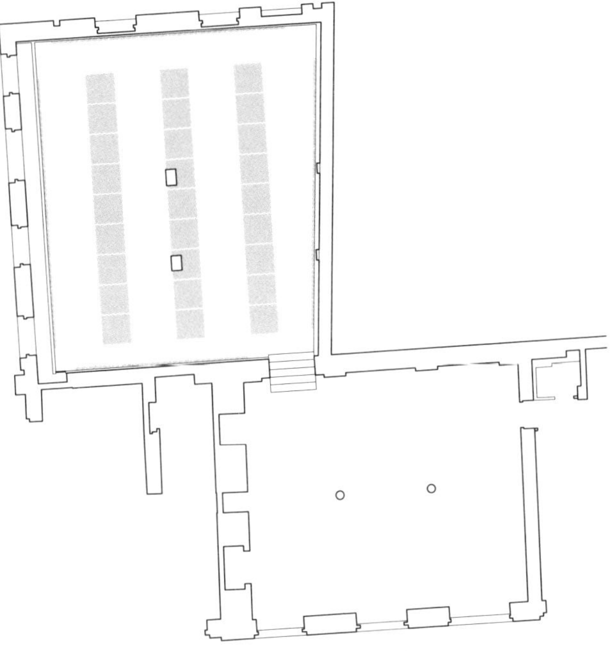

Aedes Architecture Forum, Berlin, Germany

El Paso Museum of Art, El Paso, Texas

INTRODUCTION

TATIANA BILBAO AND AYESHA S. GHOSH

This is not a book in the traditional sense: it does not have a beginning or a middle, and it most definitely does not have an ending. Imagine it as an unfinished collection of texts, a folio of sorts, that help us to grasp the incomprehensible. *Two Sides of the Border: Reimagining the Region* was, from the beginning, a method to grapple with the current divisive rhetoric about Mexico and the United States. To reimagine these two countries as a single territory is a nearly insurmountable task. The conversation has been mostly directed at the border. Although the border is where conflicts meet, the potential of thinking of Mexico and the United States as one region allows us to better understand the interweaving relationships that are cast far beyond the border region.

The only way, in our mind, to reimagine the region was trying to understand it first. Why is it divided? What history caused these two nations to be bound by tension, rather than unity? To undergo this task, we had to layer all types of stories. No one individual can give a clear picture of the situation between Mexico and the United States, because so many individuals live different social realities, while larger connections exist economically, politically and historically.

Imagination is a key player through which we approach architecture. In our office we play quite a bit with architectural representation to harness and push these early stages of imagination, not just as a fantastical act, but an exercise to solve problems, project into the future, come up with alternatives to preexisting norms, devise experiences. We draw inspiration from all forms such as nature and site analysis, as well as from paintings, poetry and art to contribute to a more complete approach to designs. We then produce images and models through collages and drawings and sketches, hoping to capture the ethos of a project before committing to concrete spaces and programs. These images we produce are layered, complex and often abstract. They become the point of conversation and discussion within our own office but also with future users. In this way, we keep ourselves open to interpretation and intuitive impulses. The layered image allows us to communicate and connect with more people in a deep way. Each person who looks at a collage will draw out the parts that connect with them the most, with which they can see themselves participating in unique ways or that much more holistically respond to their needs and desires. Working on *Two Sides of the Border* helped us realize how important the act of imagination is in identifying problems and finding solutions for issues as big as transborder politics.

We approached the *Two Sides of the Border* initiative with a collage-like methodology. Our collaborators were invited to layer their stories, research and interests to not only better understand Mexico–US relations but to imagine ways the future could be productive for people on both sides of the border. We invite a new vision of these two nations in which they are tied together by bonds of collaboration, empathy and mutual support that enhance each other. Every person is tied together by some degree of transnational issues, creating an abundance of stories, a near infinite number. This publication captures a few of those.

The *Two Sides of the Border* initiative began with a call for participation of architecture studios taught in both Mexico and the US. Deborah Berke, dean of the Yale School of Architecture, expanded the idea to include an exhibition and book, allowing for more layers, bringing in more stories. Dean Amale Andraos of GSAPP, Columbia University, also provided critical support to the endeavor, and with their support, thirteen architecture studios were taught across twelve institutions in the spring of 2018, all dealing with some aspects of Mexico–US relations. Each studio endeavored to understand the spatial implications of the relationship between the two countries through different methodologies and proposals. The proposals responded to a wide range of briefs presented by their professors, but each taking place in a site within the region. They used tools beyond traditional architecture to contribute to cross-cultural conversation. Together, the studios aggregated a multitude of stories that not only contributed to an understanding of the present situation but also imagined potential futures of the relations. Photographer Iwan Baan worked alongside the studios, traveling to each of their sites to document their environment and conditions, contributing his insightful and sensitive way of capturing people and their surroundings. Through his experience and lens we are given images of brightly colored remittance houses in Oaxaca and Puebla and the gargantuan food production hubs in Kansas. These evocative images add personal stories and a sense of relation between vastly different places.

The inaugural exhibition showcasing the student work and photographs took place in the fall of 2018 in the Yale SoA gallery with a dedicated team of fabricators and installers from the school. We worked with Nile Greenberg, with whom Tatiana had taught one of the studios at Columbia University GSAPP, to curate and organize the hundreds of proposals produced by the studios. The exhibition took on the form of an atlas, including historical maps alongside new ones that we commissioned from Thomas Paturet to accompany the student work and

Iwan's photos to create this atlas, unpacked further in Nile's introduction.

The exhibition began to travel, first to Aedes Gallery in Berlin where a conference related North American cultural climates to historical ones, the fall of the Berlin Wall 30 years ago and contemporary issues like refugees and migration in Europe. The panel brought in new perspectives, from artists practicing in Europe to regional voices like Carlos Hagerman, who contributed a piece on his documentary films about immigrant experiences to this publication. We could see the conversation getting larger: more people were able to engage because the core of what we were talking about was also relevant to their very different experiences. Questions of identity, placehood and home resonate globally. The exhibition continues to travel. Its last installation in El Paso was particularly meaningful; it was on the invitation of the Texas Tech El Paso architecture school, a participant in the academic initiative. Hosted by Ersela Kripa and Stephen Mueller, both with essays in this publication, the overlap of stories emerged even more. Collaborators in the project have had a ripple effect, inviting us into an endless network of people working on transnational issues. Alejandro Luperca, in his contribution to this publication, writes about a project he is intimately familiar with, the *Border Tuner*, an interactive apparatus by Rafael Lozano-Hemmer. Months after reading his first draft of the essay, we happened to be in El Paso to open our exhibition and were able to see the *Border Tuner* in person. High-powered lights were beaming from El Paso to Juárez and from Juárez to El Paso, unobstructed and unfazed by the geopolitical border, the beams were controllable to rotate and meet in bright white bridges. Every time the lights met, they would create a two-way real-time radio connection, carrying live voices from the other side — collapsing the space of the border and molding shared experiences out of literally thin air.

Networks of similarities and unforeseen connections emerged while working on this collection you are holding. Stories of bees are told in a piece by Carlos Zedillo and resonate with the student work of Hallie Black (Cornell University) on butterflies, both exploring transborder ecologies and bringing our perception to an insect scale. Our own preoccupation with the politics of mapmaking was enriched by Andrei Harwell's piece on the history of mapmaking, which adds a layer to Ersela Kripa's report on border walls and infrastructures of surveillance. These are just a few of the voices brought together in this publication, which alongside Iwan's bright photos and the student's insightful work, piece together a collaged image of a hopeful and unified Mexico–US region.

This publication is a part of a larger project. We are not just speaking about the Two Sides of the Border initiative, with its academic and exhibition components, but about all of the architects, artists, policy makers and everyone else who are working to create a better future for the intertwined Mexico and United States. The publication gave us the opportunity to really analyze a multitude of narratives. We invite you, our readers, to glimpse facets of a whole that we are still reaching for.

INTERVIEW

IWAN BAAN, TATIANA BILBAO, NILE GREENBERG

On July 4, 2019, I was finally able to schedule a meeting between the two very busy collaborators of this book.

I had always considered Tatiana and Iwan collaborators to some degree; they had worked on Ordos as well as Tatiana's Ruta del Peregrino in the past. What I didn't understand is that this project was their first true collaboration. It started not only with a shared political framework, but also a shared interest in capturing how architecture, cities and people all relate to one another. Their ability to share this definition of architecture is captured so well in this book and is expounded upon in this interview.

Iwan Baan was in Mexico City at the time. Tatiana Bilbao was in London. This was a long-awaited interview that we intentionally scheduled toward the end of the production of the project. The first exhibition at Yale had been staged, Iwan had given a fascinating lecture and Tatiana was working toward this book. In some ways this was one of the few moments to regroup and evaluate not just the opinions of the authors, but to come to a collective understanding of what the project was able to accomplish.

–Nile

Nile Greenberg — Thank you both for sitting down and finding time. . . . I want to ask my first big question, directed more toward you, Tatiana. The project is called, or has transformed into, Two Sides of the Border: Reimagining the Region. My question is what exactly are we reimagining, or what is our imagination in this scenario?

Tatiana Bilbao — For me, it is imagining a place where the border doesn't exist. Obviously, that is too much imagination. I think that more and more I don't believe in borders, and I think that we need to rethink borders, because as soon as you have a border, you have a limitation to everything. I think that we should erase limitations. For the sake of being optimists, I think we have advanced very much in removing a lot of borders and limits in our society, but I think we still have a lot of limitations. An important one is the notion of country borders, the definition of "country." I would like to think of this not even as erasing national borders, that would be going too far, but I do think that we can imagine or think of these as regions in a more comparative way. Right now we are living in the complete extreme of creating even more division. We would like to imagine a place where countries exist but are not relevant.

NG Directing it to you, Iwan, with regard to that same idea of imagination, I think that Tatiana chose to work with you on this project because of the ability of your photos to help us imagine both the reality of what's happening right now, as well as convey Tatiana's regional idea of imagination. Can you describe how your travels reflect or imagine some of the ideas that Tatiana is describing?

Iwan Baan For me, what was really interesting about taking on this project was working in both countries. I traveled quite extensively in both the United States and Mexico. At times, for me, it was like the border wasn't even there. You can cross it in an instant, but then you see the major difficulties for the other 99 percent of the people who have the ambition to go from Mexico to the US. In a way, the two countries are becoming very close in their goals and what they are trying to do, but there is this big border in the middle which is impossible to cross for a lot of people. Cultures start to merge; people copy what they see from the movies and try to live the idea of what families working north of the border can bring to the south of the border, the materials and the stories and the money, and so on.

The challenge was how to visualize this cultural back-and-forth across very different landscapes. If you go to Europe, all these countries are completely different and have their own identities. In the Americas, it's the same in some ways, but at the same time the different countries are also merging and equalizing. I thought it would be very interesting to look at all the different aspects of this coming together across different locations.

TB I wanted to work with Iwan because of his understanding and position of neutrality in capturing the situation. I really like how he captures these moments as they are, without filtering them through any emotional or picturesque charge. I thought it was really important to have a neutral — well, perhaps *neutral* is not the right word, that is too easily misunderstood — vision that captures things as they are without any overtly personal layers underneath the work. I think Iwan really achieves that.

IB I also went into this with a sort of blank canvas. I had heard a lot of things and had done a lot of research, but I really wanted to step into these environments with a neutralized approach. I wanted to simply see what happens and observe the cross-cultural references in both places. Things suddenly started popping up; you see how Mexicans living in the US bring the culture back to Mexico, how the economic drives of both countries become more and more equal in certain ways, but do so simultaneously across starkly different landscapes.

NG This project strikes me as different from your other collaborative projects. It doesn't focus on just one building, one target, or one route. It's trying to capture something that goes outside of architecture, or even urbanism. Iwan, your work is known for being both intimate and urban, photojournalistic in capturing people and places while simultaneously capturing an aerial view of the region. Moving between those two extremes, from the detail to the aerial, is a really interesting approach. I'm curious as to what your thoughts are on the role of photography outside of architecture.

IB I thought of these places in terms of their different landscapes and how people inhabit them, and the connections people make with others. With these aerial shots you can put a lot of things into context. Very obviously around the border you can see the stark difference between the north and south, and all the activity that goes through these border crossings where everything culminates. You also see how, in North America, in places like Ulysses, Texas, or in Cincinnati, logistics infrastructure and economic moves physically impact the landscape. These are things you can really visualize when you step away from the subjective and look at a large overview. Shooting from small airplanes is flexible. You can travel long distances to really get an overview over long stretches of land. It was interesting to see suddenly all these landscapes and cityscapes next to each other, and the differences between these places.

TB In my case, with regard to our collaboration, I think this is the first time we've really collaborated. We worked together with Ruta del Peregrino, but in this case it is completely our collaboration. I am sorry, Iwan, if you felt like you were just out in the blue by yourself, but that was part of it. As I said, I really wanted your unique perspective. The fact that you are not Mexican was very important. I think it is very difficult when you have to be one or the other. There are always biases because we, as Mexicans, have lived our whole lives with the subject of the border. They asked me to do a piece for the AA (Architectural Association) about the border, and I explained that the first time I realized there was a border was when I could not get a visa for the US for more than 10 days because my grandfather was a Communist. Well, for them, he was. My grandfather had been a minister of the government of La República in Spain, and was therefore classified by the US as a Communist, so we couldn't get a visa for more than 10 days. That was the first time I realized there was a border, and the border meant the impossibility of crossing for more than 10 days, and having to explain to the US what I was going to do during my 10-day visit. I really have lived my whole life with this idea of a border with the US, so it was important to have someone at the core of this project who has not grown up with that cultural charge.

NG Now that the project and its photography is complete, assuming you had some hypothesis or expectation, is there something, Tatiana, that you've discovered from the project so far that you didn't know or understand previously?

TB That is a difficult question. There are many things that I came to realize more fully. For example, when we were researching remittance houses, I realized the degree to which NAFTA affected the construction industry, the way it physically impacted the Mexican landscape. After living through the earthquake and the reconstruction that came after, I came to understand that the imported building materials had only been in Mexico for a short time, and workers didn't really know how to use them. They tried to use them according to an image of another place, but didn't have actual familiarity with them.

IB I saw that agreements like NAFTA literally impact the landscape in these places. I especially saw this from the air. The aerial photographs show how these massive industrial areas around the border developed. You can see the physical effects of economic changes in the shipping industry around Cincinnati and Texas. You think it is just an economic agreement, but it has a major impact also on the landscapes of different places.

NG The two examples you're giving are really some of the most powerful images in the project, remittance houses and the infrastructure around the border. It's interesting that they are both results of NAFTA in a moment when the world is reevaluating multinational ties, like the EU, for example. We're wondering what is going to happen to those very powerful places and transnational agreements.

TB On one hand we are questioning but holding on to values that we have been pursuing for centuries, and on the other hand, we are trying to let go of everything. We haven't found a neat way to do either of those things, and therefore we have a binary story and not a story that flows easily. My dream would be to think that there are no more borders. I think that is the future. The future goes back to the moment where there were cities. Empires were founded with the power of cities. I don't know how soon that will happen. Maybe we won't see that in our lifetime?

IB I don't know. I saw this statistic that when the Berlin Wall fell, there were 16 border fences around the world, and nowadays there are almost 65 in the last 30 years. It's going in the opposite direction. Traveling is getting easier and easier for one percent of the world's population. You and I have no problems crossing any borders, but for the other 99 percent, these borders are becoming way more problematic than before.

NG Talking about the Berlin Wall, maybe it's important to talk about the current US border wall. Iwan, the border and the US border wall prototypes were one of your primary sites in your travels. This project proposes a counterimage to the need that people have to hear that there is a wall, whether it's doing anything or not. How does this project counter that dialogue?

IB Seeing the border and the wall prototypes from the air puts it in such a perspective, seeing this massive density on the south side of the wall and this little fence that's trying to hold it back. I think it's a metaphor for what we are experiencing these days. Like Tatiana says, I hope these walls will be over soon, because it just doesn't make any sense to have them in this region. It's really just this thin line, in a sense. It comes out especially when you view these places from far away.

NG If we agree that there is a very powerful and compelling image of that wall, then there's a flip side to that wherein we believe in the incredible power of architecture to create new imaginations, to build new narratives about countries. I'm curious, Tatiana, how does architecture, even though it is not the primary subject, play a role in your project?

TB I obviously don't believe that architecture can solve the problems of the world. Architecture is not solely responsible for finding solutions to the political issues of the world, but I believe it can definitely have an impact. I don't think we can change the course of what's happening, and architecture definitely will not change countries and all of the sudden erase borders. I think what architecture can do is understand the situation and create more possibilities toward that goal.

Going back to the time when architects were really thinking about the territory is what we need. I think we have lost that opportunity in the last decades of the twentieth century and the first decades of this century. Architects have moved away from thinking territorially in big movements, with a focus on planning and an understanding of society. They have done so in favor of focusing on the individual project and the potential for garnering acclaim for changing neighborhoods. It should be the other way around. We should think of how that territory changes people and therefore create a new architecture.

NG I think that's great. One of the exciting parts of this project is how you brought in 129 students to participate in the Two Sides of the Border studios. They were exposed to your notion of territorial, interrelated architecture, especially on the topic of the border. Tatiana, how did you develop this project, starting with teaching and then the exhibition and then the book and Iwan's project. . . . How will all these different formats impact on the current generation and on the next generation?

TB To start with, my concern came from the problem of reducing all the discourse to the concept of a border, a line. I don't think understanding the relationship between the United States and Mexico can be defined by a line. The line is always what directly confronts the issues, and it carries a powerful charge, but I think the issues are much broader. The key moment of the project was opening the process of understanding that these issues happen in Mérida, in San Francisco, or in Ulysses, Arkansas, Chicago, and not only in the hyperconfronted El Paso and Ciudad Juárez. If we are able to understand that these issues are closer to us than we think, we won't simply think of the relationship between the United States and Mexico in terms of a border. If we begin to think of that relationship in a quotidian way, in an everyday way, in every spoonful of soup that you bring to your mouth, we will be able to relate and understand it more. Then we will be able to work toward something that is better for everybody.

My hesitation to do something about this situation came when the current president of the United States was elected. One of the most important reasons he was elected was his approach and his discourse toward Mexico. I was very shocked to find that almost half of the US population would go for that discourse. I think that the only way this happened is due to a huge lack of knowledge of what the relationship between the US and Mexico means.

I hate to reduce this to that very stupid movie, *A Day Without Mexicans*, but if you actually think about what would happen on a day with no Mexicans in the US, you wouldn't vote for the person saying these things. We need to really reconsider a lot of things. I can only spread the word of my field, of my surroundings. This is why I thought of initiating this project, and why I decided to create a broader spectrum by involving other people and more universities. I wanted to make the point that it's not only about the line of the border. It's about everyday issues that apply to the population of the US and to the population of Mexico.

NG That makes sense. A more practical question would be, going through this process from an academic project, what are the next steps? How did you imagine each portion of the project? So we have it on record, how did the exhibition begin, and the book and the other aspects of the project?

TB As I said, I thought it was very important to involve more minds in this project. First of all, if there are more minds thinking on this subject, there will be more people spreading the word. Secondly, and most importantly, you have more diverse perspectives. For me, this has always been very important to have multiple perspectives in every project I do. In this case specifically, I do think the only reason people agree with the current political discourse is due to a lack of knowledge. Getting more people involved is the only way to create this knowledge. From the beginning, I thought it was necessary to involve a lot of people in order to create content enough for an important body of work.

The exhibition actually did not originate with me; it was it was more Deborah Berke's idea. When I first presented the project at Yale, I was worried about the reaction of my peers. I thought, "Yeesh! What did I say wrong," but immediately after I finished, Deborah grabbed me and told me that we must do an exhibition of this project, that it would be very important. I always had the idea of creating a publication and a symposium, but I had never foreseen the idea of an exhibition. I was never the one pushing for it. When it came together, definitely with the key help of you both, I shared the results at Yale and thought it was important to figure out how to move it to more places. The book was always about the necessity to have a document that could really become a compilation of materials that would end up becoming just one drop in this discursive sea. I think this is just one drop, but with every drop the sea becomes bigger. The project is just a compilation of different imaginations that comprehend the relationship between Mexico and the US. The project is meant to be a kick or a seed of something that becomes bigger and broader, that enriches by the minute the conversation that favors a region, politically speaking, rather than two countries with a border.

NG It's fortunate that the exhibition has been traveling to countries with very clear relationships with walls. First it went to Berlin for the 30-year anniversary of the wall falling, and now it is en route to El Paso where it will be literally hundreds of feet from the delineation of the two countries.

IB Yes, it's very exciting to know that it's going there. It's perfect.

NG Hopefully we will take it to Mexico as well, so that the exhibition itself is really without borders. Iwan, you have probably seen more of the border and of these locations than anyone involved. I know that Tatiana has traveled a lot, but the specific places you went followed a very precise route of certain zones of interest, conflict, shared dialogue and everyday life. You also went to some of the grittiest locations. You saw the child separation camps, the border construction zones. You crossed many checkpoints. You experienced so much of this region from the perspective of each professor participating. I am just curious about how you came away from this project with such a powerful itinerary?

IB I wanted to look at this wide variety of places all in a similar way, zooming into very personal portraits of people living in these different places. I wanted to capture their aspirations, what they are building, what they are living for, what they are working for, but I also wanted to create a grand overview of these different landscapes. I tried to tie these very different places together. When you zoom in to these different portraits of these people living in these places, it becomes a more personal story.

I was also thinking how I would approach such a project in Europe, or in other places, but here in the US and in Mexico I felt that these places shared so many commonalities in terms of their aspirations and how they live in a time of these big economic changes — and in terms of how they designed and developed their places. I wanted to tie the whole story together and see the Americas, rather than a view of Mexico and a separate view of the United States.

NG You are describing a shared view of the world, but what exactly is shared between the two countries? I think that's a good question for both of you.

IB I was amazed by the hurdles and aspirations of people on either side. In Mexico, people want to live like those people in the United States who really cannot live without Mexico. That drive is what really ties these countries together — and in a way it is why it is so ridiculous to have a border between these two countries that are so intertwined and close together. That commonality was something that really struck me when visiting all these different places.

TB To start, we share a physical environment. It is one country, one piece of land. It is not divided by anything except a political border. There is no sea between them; not even the river goes the whole way. I think that also we share a very important history. Almost half of the territory of the US belonged to Mexico not so long ago, about 130 years ago, they would have been Mexicans! They were Mexicans when Mexico was created 220 years ago. That really creates a special bond that exists. The other thing is that, if you think about the native people from the US and from Mexico . . . they have been there longer than the powerful people in the US are saying. That's also something to consider.

Recently we share a very important history, which is an economical history wherein we cannot be divided. These two countries cannot just say "Okay, let's forget about it and build a wall and that's it. We won't talk to each other anymore." It doesn't work like that.

IB Also, all these things are so recent. In my travels I had some former students helping me, showing me these places. A number of them were from Mexico, all in their 20s and early 30s, and they were telling stories about growing up in these places, describing how there was hardly a border 20 years ago. It's only recently that the border became so hard and so impenetrable for a lot of people. I think that's something quite incredible when you consider the long history of these two countries and the blip of time that we live in with all this rhetoric, and the ways in which it's become so problematic.

NG This is a useful segue to discuss the way that the time frame is speeding up with all these changes. This project is a very big idea and has a very big ambition with a long duration of thought and care, but at the moment, I think we are in a crisis. We are in a serious crisis — depending on how you think of that word — in which children are being imprisoned in horrible conditions. We have some of the worst surveillance-state behavior occurring between these two countries. Besides the long-term vision of this project, what in your opinion is happening right now, and how does this project advance your goals in that regard?

TB I do believe totally that there is a crisis in this moment. As I said, I think that the biggest division —

NG I wouldn't say that it's a migration crisis. It's a policing crisis, right?

TB It's a political crisis. The problem is that politicians are creating this crisis. The media and politicians are to blame. The media has put their finger in the fire, which is perfect. The fact that the media is involved is not a problem in itself, but if you look at the statistics showing the amount of deportations that took place during the Obama presidency, you will see that it is higher than the amount of deportations that are happening now. The crisis we are living in now is a crisis of discourse. You can see how powerful the words of this discourse are. This is a big crisis. What we need to understand is that at this moment there are probably fewer horrible things happening now, if you can say that. On one hand, they are doing things to capture people's attention. They are, for example, separating children from their families and other horrible things, but these things were already happening before.

NG I guess my question is, does this project help this discourse? How does this project improve the discourse? Iwan, how do your photos and the larger compilation of all the conversations and media associated with this project directly counter the immediate discourse of crisis?

IB I think what I try to show is that these places are so close to each other and that this crisis is almost a made-up thing in a way. These two different worlds are so close to each other and so similar in many ways. You hear the stories from the younger generation who grew up 20 years ago hardly without a border. Of course there was a border, but people from Juárez played with their friends in El Paso and the other way around. There was hardly a border crossing, and people went back and forth without passports. Now it has become this whole public spectacle. The news has taken over politics, and I hope showing the region as almost one place gives people something to think about, that these places are not so different.

NG From both of your perspectives, given the fact that borders in general are at the top of so many political conversations across the whole world right now, what do you think about the global importance of borders as far-right politicians gain power.

TB Personally, I believe there is a moment of negotiation between letting all the borders go and not letting go of any of the borders. This is a moment people are living in everywhere in the world. Obviously, everyone is afraid of letting everything go. I do think that there needs to be a certain level of control. I'm not suggesting that we simply free everything from political institutions and economic markets. I think that we are in a moment wherein we need to understand that there should be a free choice for everyone within certain rules. We have to define those certain rules that have been blurred, because capitalism has blurred some of these rules so that they do not correspond to the majority of a population. I think we are in a moment of crisis in many ways across the whole world, and certain pressures have been put specifically on borders.

NG Iwan, what do you think? You've been to more of these borders and countries than almost anyone.

IB It is so difficult because I can travel and cross all these places so easily. It's like there are so many places where these borders are such artificial things put up. We are so privileged to be able to see all of these different places in such a short amount of time, and not have so many problems crossing and working in different places. It's interesting that in the last 20 years there has been a big push to open up all these places, to remove borders in Europe and other places, but in the last

2–3 years there has been a huge backlash and there are more borders than before. You see it everywhere in the world. You see it in Europe. You see it in Asia, especially in places like Hong Kong and China. You see it here in the US. Borders are becoming such flashpoints everywhere. After establishing the idea of globalization with open borders, things seem to be moving in a completely different direction.

NG I have one last big question. What is the power of home, like hometowns, home countries, the home itself? That was the focus in both of your studios, Tatiana. Both studios are someone's home or housing. What is the relationship between your project's central topics and the idea of home?

TB First, I want to return to what Iwan was saying. I think the ability to travel so much in the last 20 years has exploded, but it has exploded for a very small percent of the population. I feel like there are almost no borders for me because I hold a passport that opens borders all over the place, because I am Spanish. If I didn't have that, it would be different. For example, a colleague of mine has the same opportunities that I have, but now she's really stuck in the middle of a situation where she cannot teach because she has a Mexican passport. And I can teach because I have a Spanish passport, even though we have the same credentials, the same opportunities, have studied in the same universities. In a way, she may have more opportunities because she comes from a very established family in Mexico that has a lot of power and wealth. I don't. I come from a family of refugees and immigrants, but in a way I have more freedom than she has, only because she was born in a different geographical place. It's very difficult. This is why I think countries should disappear.

I also think that the idea of home is superimportant in this project, because I believe that we should go back to the possibility of being able to relate to a smaller amount of people. I don't understand how a person can really be the president and represent more than 300,000,000 people. It is impossible to be a representative of so many people. We need to go back and relate to our own smaller communities, starting with a steadier relationship within our unit, a more integrated and comprehensive relationship within our neighborhoods. Then we might be able to think a little more broadly. This is why I think we will go back to a moment with no countries, when there were communities that had the potential to become empires.

IB It's also so difficult when you see these places and how people are displaced, looking for work and a life abroad, especially people from Mexico immigrating to the US. They are sending all of their earnings back to Mexico and building these remittance houses as their ideal of home. It's so difficult to combine these thoughts, because they are building their life in the United States but still have ambitions for a life in Mexico, to go back to how it used to be a long time ago in Mexico where they could build a country house for themselves and their family. How can you reconcile the idea of a home and a local environment with the circumstances of a superglobalized world? I don't have an answer. It is fascinating to see how these forces are shaping the whole continent.

NG Part of me is thinking that more and more we won't have the luxury of what Tatiana is saying about starting with communities in neighborhoods in cities. That luxury is fading given the issues of climate change and economic inequality. Mobility is going to have to be part of it. I know you have been suggesting that mobility is the answer to this question, but I'm wondering what will happen when we lose these communities, or how we will repair those relationships? That could be an upcoming problem, I'd say.

Well, we can wrap up with that in mind. Do you have any questions for one another, any questions you haven't been asked yet?

TB Hmm. Well, Iwan, when you presented the work, I was very surprised and saw things in a completely different perspective and that was very interesting, but I think you've answered most of the questions that I had for you.

IB What was the change of perspective for you?

TB I really liked that you did it from east to west, and not from north and south, one side to the other. You begin to see a continuity across all these places. You created the opportunity to see new topics and discourses and the possibility of seeing it as a region.

Did you have any questions for me?

IB For me the whole project was a brilliant eye-opener, and I was very happy to be part of it, to bring these two sides together. I tried to do that by going east to west or west to east, because thinking in terms of north and south creates the division between two countries. I felt in so many instances that there was so much overlap and so many similarities. I wanted to find a way to show how intertwined these places are, and that we all live with the same ambitions and goals and dreams on either side. There are of course huge economic inequalities, but at the same time, we're also all the same in a way.

NG We can leave it there. Thank you both very much. And thank you so much for doing this project! It's great!

TB Yes, thank you!

IB Yes, this was very nice. Thank you.

THE TRAVELING SERIALIZED
ADVENTURES OF KID QUIXOTE

STEPHEN HAFF

BUSHWICK, NEW YORK

74.00°

At Still Waters in a Storm, Stephen Haff has been holding in-depth reading classes every Saturday for kids in Bushwick, Brooklyn. While attending one of those classes, which is usually accompanied by a round of pizzas, one might encounter an impromptu soccer match, playful teenage drama or incredibly close readings of *Don Quixote* or Jorge Luis Borges's "The Library of Babel." These classes have been conducted in various forms for more than a decade and work especially with children from Mexico and Central America who live in the neighborhood. The children who attend Stephen's class are very present and active and are always seen and heard by one another. Presented in the following excerpts are a selection of songs written as a translation of *Don Quixote*, but reconstructing the story as children traveling across Mexico and into the United States because, as a song explains, "innocence needs a home."

— Nile

"THE BELIEVING SONG"

CHORUS [sings]:
DE CLARO EN CLARO
DE TURBIO EN TURBIO
LEYENDO, IMAGINANDO Y CREYENDO

FROM STARLIGHT TO STARLIGHT
FROM SHADOW TO SHADOW
READING, IMAGINING AND BELIEVING

"RESCUING SONG"

VERSE 1:
BOY:
I BEG YOU TO UNDERSTAND ME
TO LISTEN TO MY VOICE
I'M NOT ASKING TO BE REVERED, HERE
I JUST WANT TO HAVE A CHOICE
I JUST WANT TO HAVE A CHOICE
POR FAVOR, ENTIÉNDAN ME!
IGNORANCE BUILT THIS WALL.
I DON'T WANT TO LIVE IN FEAR
MI FAMILIA IS MY BEST OF ALL.

CHORUS:
CAN WE HELP? CAN WE HELP? CAN WE HELP?
WE WILL PROTECT YOU WITH OUR SONG.
CAN WE HELP? CAN WE HELP? CAN WE HELP?
WE FEEL DEEP IN OUR HEARTS YOU BELONG.

VERSE 2:
BOY:
I CAME HERE TO SEEK PROTECTION
I TRAVELED THROUGH THE NIGHT
ADIOS PRECIOSA PATRIA
FOUND MYSELF IN BURNING LIGHT
BURNING BURNING DESERT LIGHT
POR FAVOR, ENTIÉNDAN ME!
NOBODY WANTS YOUR THRONE
WE'RE NOT GOING TO STEAL YOUR GOLD
BUT INNOCENCE NEEDS A HOME

CHORUS:
CAN WE HELP? CAN WE HELP? CAN WE HELP?
WE'LL WIPE THE DUST OFF OF YOUR FACE.
CAN WE HELP? CAN WE HELP? CAN WE HELP?
LIFT YOU UP, TAKE YOU HOME, AND EMBRACE.

"ADVENTUROUS ADVENTURE SONG"

VERSE 1:
QUIXOTE:
I PROMISE SOFT GROUND BENEATH OUR FEET
WALKING ON GRASS INSTEAD OF THE STREET
CARTWHEELS, PINWHEELS, PLAYING IN THE RAIN
MAKING OUR OWN WORLD, EVEN BROCCOLI WILL BE SWEET

OUR CLASSROOM WILL BE ALL OF SPAIN
RIDING THE WIND LIKE A PAPER AIRPLANE
ROLLER COASTERS, L TRAIN, DISCOVER WHAT YOU'VE NEVER TRIED
OUR ADVENTURES WILL BE CROWNED WITH GLORY AND FAME

CHORUS:
ADVENTUROUS ADVENTURE SONG
VA-MO-NOS!
ADVENTUROUS ADVENTURE SONG
VA-MO-NOS!
ADVENTUROUS ADVENTURE SONG
VA-MO-NOS!
WE'RE GOING ON AN ADVENTURE!

AVENTUROSA CANCIÓN AVENTUROSA
LET'S GO!
AVENTUROSA CANCIÓN AVENTUROSA
LET'S GO!
AVENTUROSA CANCIÓN AVENTUROSA
LET'S GO!
NOS VAMOS A UNA AVENTURA!

“CANCIÓN DESESPERADA”

GRISÓSTOMO [sings]:
DEL LOBO FIERO
EL TEMEROSO AULLIDO,
Y EL ESTRUENDO DEL VIENTO
CONTRASTADO EN MAR INSTABLE;
Y DE LA VIUDA TORTOLILLA
EL SENSIBLE ARRULLAR;
MEZCLADOS EN UN SON
PARA RECONTAR MI PENA CRUEL

YO MUERO, YO MUERO, YO MUERO!
OFRECERÉ A LOS VIENTOS CUERPO Y ALMA

[MARCELA appears, above]

TÚ! TÚ! TÚ! TÚ ERES
LA RAZÓN QUE ME FUERZA
A VIVIR UNA VIDA QUE ABORRESZCO

DEL LOBO FIERO
EL TEMEROSO AULLIDO,
Y EL ESTRUENDO DEL VIENTO
CONTRASTADO EN MAR INSTABLE;
Y DE LA VIUDA TORTOLILLA
EL SENSIBLE ARRULLAR;

DESESPERADO!
DESESPERADO!
DESESPERADO!

"RULER OF MYSELF SONG"

INTRODUCTION

MARCELA:
I WANT TO LOVE WHO I LOVE
DREAM WHAT I WANT TO DREAM
FEEL THE WIND AS IF IT'S MY FREEDOM
I WANT TO UNDERSTAND THIS FRIGHTENED LITTLE GIRL
AM I THE RULER OF MYSELF?

VERSE 1:
AM I TOO YOUNG?
I AM AFRAID
WHERE DO I GO?
WILL I BE BRAVE?
WHERE IS MY PATH?
WHO WILL I FOLLOW?
DO I HAVE TO FOLLOW?
AM I THE RULER OF MYSELF?

BRIDGE:
I BELIEVE IN HUGS
PEOPLE STUCK TOGETHER LIKE THE PETALS OF A ROSE
EN MI FAMILIA DE DIENTES DE LEÓN
GROWING LOVE FOR EVERYONE
I BELIEVE EVERYONE SHOULD FEEL LOVED
NO MATTER THEIR
LOOKS, LANGUAGE, IDIOMA
CAPACIDAD, RAZA, RELIGION
NO MATTER THEIR
COUNTRY, STATUS, DINERO OR DIFFERENCE
ORIENTACIÓN
ANYTHING AT ALL
UN JARDÍN DE FLORES DE TODOS LOS AMORES
WHO DECIDES IF A FLOWER IS A WEED?
AM I THE RULER OF MYSELF?

VERSE 2:
[EVERYONE]:
WE CHOOSE TO LOVE HOW
WE LOVE
BELIEVE IN WHAT WE
DREAM
FEEL THE WIND AND FEEL
OUR FREEDOM
I AM NO LONGER THAT
FRIGHTENED LITTLE GIRL
I AM THE RULER OF MYSELF

CONCLUSION
[EVERYONE]:
YES I AM YOUNG
AND I AM BRAVE
AND I WILL GO
WHERE INJUSTICE GOES
AND I WILL STAY
FOR THOSE WHO NEED MY
HELP
SOY VALIENTE!
YO SE MI PROPÓSITO
Y DOMINO MI DESTINO
I AM THE RULER
I AM THE RULER

INTERVIEW WITH PARTICIPANTS TERREMOTO

NEW YORK CITY, NEW YORK 74.00°

One of the unfortunate necessities of being the editor for this atlas is having to reduce incredibly thoughtful work by 129 students to a handful of pages. I had spent a semester myself with six of these students at Columbia University, each with such a strong sense of their own work. When Diego Del Valle and I first discussed the project, I was taken aback by his heavy criticism of the students' work, language and images. It was quite intense and had a precise political energy that seemed unfair to the students without knowing them. After an internal conversation between us, we decided that a conversation would be a more successful approach. I assured Diego that if he spoke to these students, they would have already considered and factored in many of his remarks to their projects that was larger than any singular issue. From there we conducted these fascinating and enlightening interviews and in the end, Diego's prompts were a useful check on the often internalized nature of architecture.

— Nile

"Whom did you design this project for?" is an elemental question for architectural practice. When designing architectural projects, the answer to this question unfolds reflections that tense the distance between the singular individuality of the architect and that community that is intended to inhabit it. This question was the starting point to trigger conversations with Nikki Weitz, Tonia Chi Sing, Marilyn Reyes and Hallie Black, some of the students who were part of the collaborations that are compiled in this book. We present here some extracts of these conversations about their experience of collaboration in these architectural projects to stop and reflect about the possibility of architecture's moving away from developmentalist policies that perpetuate colonial relations with territories.

When Nile invited me to collaborate, I received the PDF of each project to familiarize myself with them. The first thing I noticed was the coldness of the language that formed them. From the black-and-white renders to the descriptions, a rigidity obscured the fictional possibilities of presenting the combination of text and image related to the projection of a space where life was supposed to happen. Thus, it made me think on the importance of valuing and questioning language in relation to the power of architecture as an exercise of imagination of the world and the implications that this entails in making visible the possibilities of inhabiting that world. Since any idea is always woven in relation to and with others, architecture needs to reclaim its exercise of imagination beyond its relation to the construction industry and the hyperaccelerated logics of capitalism behind it.

— Diego Del Valle

Nikki Weitz

Diego Del Valle Whom did you design this project for?

Nikki Weitz Looking at underutilized industrial space, this project is for citizens around large infrastructural sites drawing attention to the in-between spaces that form in neighborhoods located next to large warehouses that are part of the food system complex.

DV What about those people who are not considered citizens in the US?

NW Maybe *citizens* isn't the best word. We were thinking in terms of residents whose housing is near these construction and industrial sites related to food production. The industrial infrastructure that architecture builds for food industry is related directly to the way in which our groceries get to our local store. How to blur the lines that limit the organization of this space and its relation with daily life?

The collaborative aspect of having a group of people looking at very specific instances on the borders related to local, national and international food systems made me realize how reliant we are on each other. Understanding the interactions that make possible, for example, the transportation of food miles away taking into account the waste that goes into it, made me question: What if those connections were paused and that's the instance we started to work in?

DV You are proposing a deacceleration, which in relation to architecture means a political practice of degrowth, which, in your project, is about a food industry system responding directly to capitalist expansion. Any thoughts?

NW In architecture we have all these categories, rigid constraints that divide and organize any kind of space possibility. Hybridizing those categories could be a way of degrowth. Although "hybridize" isn't necessarily something that I used in this project, I was reassembling: taking these stereotypical assemblies of a warehouse and reworking its structural elements as an industrial building to allow other things to happen.

Nile Greenberg Your point is that there is some problem with typology. The warehouses, for instance, are extremely dependent on migrant labor. Those typologies between the social and the construction/design aspect end up being deeply segregated. The whole industry — and its entire supply chain — is actually invisible by design. It's also a place where migrant labor tasked with this food production would meet people who live in the largely segregated city. They would end up connecting on some level.

NW This actually translated into my thesis the following year. I continued to look into the migrant worker condition in my region of Ohio. I ended up carrying it on, looking into how food is produced and what the architectural standards are for a small-town farm. I ended up designing a farmhouse that integrates migrant workers and their families. I guess my reflection was carrying that study on and looking harder at who is growing the food for whom in our region, and how does that translate internationally? Who are we facilitating to come into this region to help us produce the food and do the work that we can't keep up with on our own at the current pace? It was a matter of facilitating these international exchanges to tackle the segregation that we have in the region.

Marilyn Reyes

DV Whom did you design this project for?

Marilyn Reyes This project was thought in relation to the migration trajectories of monarch butterflies, to help them have a space to rest in the borderlands between MX and the US as migrant nonhuman creatures within a border infrastructure. A fence is pointless for migrant creatures that fly.

When I started working in the Rio Valley, I wanted the project to be away from traffic and people. I really didn't incorporate humans into it. It could function as a space for people to get out of the heat or rest, but ultimately it doesn't have places for humans.

NG So, it's best to describe it as "not for humans," basically.

DV In this contrast between human and nonhuman architecture in the context of the US-MX border, what was your experience working collaboratively with the studio and how do you frame your project as part of that?

MW It was contrasting to talk with people who were not very familiar with the US-Mexican border. They didn't really understand how one can't just cross in the same way. The militarized border implies different dynamics than that from Canada. Canadians from the studio have different perspectives and experiences of border crossing, relate to having a bridge to get from one country to the other. Those different views helped us develop our project.

Personally, it was a little different, because I was very unfamiliar with the region. I was born in El Paso, but I was raised in Juárez. People from the studio had more opportunities to imagine, and thereon build something across the border within that region, an experience that the US-Mexican border doesn't really offer.

Regarding nonhuman architecture, it was different from their focus because they were used to working on traditional architecture and designs for humans. When I was working on my project, I had to explain that my focus was the opposite; it was only for migratory creatures, not human migration. Nonhuman architecture in some way is easier because you don't have to deal with all the traditional building codes or traditional architectures; however, it was also a challenge because it's very difficult to design something that you're not familiar with. We can explore, and we can research and try to understand how monarch butterflies travel, but we, as humans will never experience it. Traditional architecture focuses on space within human interaction. It's more difficult to design for animals because we don't know how they will interact with the space or if the design will work or not for this purpose. During the collaborative process we had conversations about the challenge in designing for a different audience, in this case insects.

DV What if humans started occupying this space? And from there, what are the limitations of the project?

MW Human occupation would be great! We could help the project to have different purposes in that sense. It had the purpose of helping creatures and insects, but it could also be a shelter for humans. It has what a human could use to survive as a space to escape the heat of the desert, and it's an enclosed area near the border. Although, limitations involved finding the right location to build this, away from traffic and dense human activity, a green area, which are very limited along the border. Another limitation, of course, was the fence. Could this be an apolitical infrastructure? Because we have a nonhuman audience, it creates an opportunity to have a nonpolitical space or infrastructure.

DV In that sense it is very political. It's political in the way that it's questioning the nationalist development of the border related to necropolitics. It's a very symbolic and poetic understanding of architecture.

NG Design-wise, you're sort of making a social monument to architecture that changes the way we consider the militarized aesthetic. How do you feel about using and appropriating militarized design forms, such as the edge and the point, to create a space that is also intentionally nonhuman?

DV From that question, and following the power of fictionalization when imagining an architectural project, how do you feel about the possibility of militarized groups occupying the space after being attracted by the militarized aesthetics?

MW The design plays a really important role in imagining a space that doesn't welcome humans. I was trying to imagine an apolitical structure where only creatures and not humans were invited to this space.

The military occupation is a possibility, a real conflict. I don't want them to use the space. That would be a terrible thing to happen. We already have a fence and a military infrastructure watching that space from both sides.

NG I think the design for your project changes the very bad connotation of military aesthetics into something much more beautiful. That's an advantage of your project; the power of fictionalization in that case lies in it.

Tonia Chi Sing

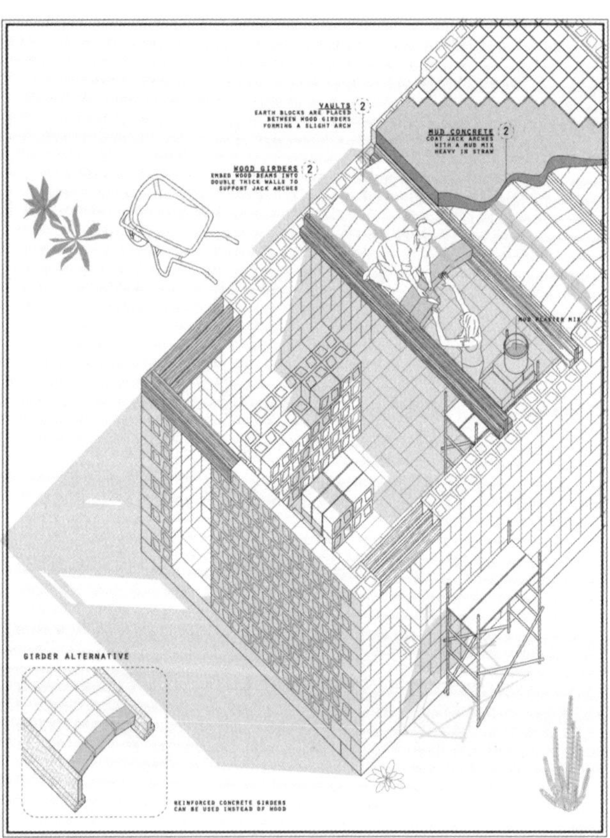

DV Whom did you design this project for? It's clear that it is designed for specific social communities in the rural landscape of Mexico, thereon, we would like to know more about the used language and images that create this manual. Who are the people that will be reading it?

Tonia Chi Sing The manual is much more about a basis for beginning a relationship or a conversation with communities that are living in these rural areas in Mexico where remittance homes are commonly built.

In our previous email exchange, Diego, you asked: "why not make the manual with the communities themselves rather than making a manual to give to them?" I completely agree with that. I think that if I were to actually do this manual outside of the vacuum of this studio environment, this very condensed three-month academic prompt, I would be spending a lot of time visiting and building relationships with the communities that I would potentially be working with.

When I put this manual together, it was more about creating a way for me to think about my own perceptions of the issues that I perceived. I examined what I understood as perceived challenges for some of these communities, as well as the principles that I might pair with some of these perceived challenges. It was more of a tool to be self-aware of my own ideas, my own beliefs and my own knowledge. If I were to take this into a scenario wherein I'd be putting this manual out there as a resource for communities, it would have to be much more of a collaborative process. It's not for the community as an end product, but as a means toward a potential end product in the future.

NG I'm curious as to how you think of your project as a part of this collaborative initiative. How do you think the collaboration went as a whole?

TS It's great that this collaborative initiative is translated into a book and an exhibition. Although, the audience of these are not going to be those communities; the audience is people like us.

I don't know if within that same initiative there is a desire to bring the project into other realms where we're actually working directly with some of the communities that we're talking about, to see what their reactions are to our thoughts about them. I think that would be an interesting additional dimension.

I think that it's important that we're talking about it amongst ourselves, of course. Architecture is more and more shifting toward social practice, as this initiative makes evident. I am curious as to whether some of these continued collective efforts will become collective across communities as well as the professionals that have been involved.

DV The distance you described between the academic realm, where the conception of the project happens, and the actual communities and social context in which this project is thought to be implemented, was something very evident for me when reading the PDFs of the projects.

An in-between lines affirmative jargon that proposes the project as a truth revealed a distance between the imagination of the architect and the actual context. Do you have any reflection about how architecture and practice is tackling or being self-reflective in those terms, or even in your own practice in relation to this project?

TS This is definitely something that I think about a lot. I think my first reaction to this was, "What is the point of talking about this continuously in this context?" We aren't really closing that gap or that distance. We're just talking amongst ourselves. I think that is one of the biggest issues. We're only talking amongst ourselves. I think it would be beneficial if we all talked about the process more, instead of a product.

I think that is one of the challenges of my manual. I'm producing this product that's supposed to be mass-distributed. It's almost like it's disseminating these elitist architectural values to this community. That is not at all what I intend for my book. I would never produce this manual and distribute it to people in rural Mexico. I would be embarrassed to do so. It's not that I wouldn't show them. I would absolutely show them, but I wouldn't ask them to check out this amazing thing that I know about that they should also know. I don't want it to be something that I've just come up with, without any of their input.

I don't really know what to do about the fact that Western academia ideals or ways of thinking have undervalued other ways of thinking and understanding. I think the first step is being aware of how we impact knowledge that is not Western-oriented. I think that the more transparent we are about our doubts, the more we will be able to close that division and be able to actually listen to the people. That being said, that possibility also exists in this ideal, perfect world wherein everyone has time to sit around and talk to each other about these things. A lot of the time, people in these communities just want to get their house built and live in it. They don't want to have a long conversation about what this means. It's just like the rest of us. We just want to have our basic needs taken care of.

DV Also, there's this national relation in which the whole collaborative project was conceived. The diplomatic bilateral aspect of it is conceived from a class privilege in which those who get to create the discourse of this relation, in other words, those who are in this book, are people who are not affected by that relation in terms of daily living. How, in this collaborative experience, can the discipline of architecture help decolonize space projection and space building?

TS I think one way would be to not impose your values and your ideals onto communities. In architecture we do that a lot, unfortunately. It is a colonial habit in detriment of the communities themselves and the adaptability of their cultures. Specifically with earthen architecture, there is a lot of interest in kind of rewriting these traditions that have been lost through the first wave of these colonial attitudes. At this point, I think that it's very important to be aware of the risk of replaying that by making connections where they may not be present.

For instance, a lot of these communities don't really build with earth anymore. They build with cinder blocks. They don't necessarily feel connected to earth as a building tradition. That isn't the case everywhere, but that is the case in a lot of these places. I think that it is important for us to be aware of conflating the culturally appropriate with contextual realities. You may see earthen buildings around, but maybe culturally the community doesn't necessarily relate to that method anymore. It doesn't mean that they may or may not in the future. I think that being aware of your biases is one of the important things. As an architect or as a professional, when you make decisions, you don't make them in a vacuum. When you build in a certain way, you think in terms of what material will be used in building? It's not prescriptive. What are the factors that you're considering? What is the cost? Where are the materials coming from? What kind of climate are you in? There are all these things that you think about when you assess how you're going to build something.

I think that sharing that knowledge is more useful than saying, "I concluded from my own calculations in my own head from my own training that this is how it should be done. You should build with earth, because it's local and it's part of your tradition. It's the better way to do this." I think that not being so prescriptive would be a good first step in the endeavor to decolonize architectural practice. I think it's an important question we should think about more as architects.

Hallie Black

DV Your project is one of the most challenging in terms of understanding the architecture beyond its usual implications. It's very abstract. The structure of your project is floating all around. This sums up a lot of ideas that have been popping up in our previous conversations with other students about imagination and fictionalization in architectural practice.

Hallie Black Well, the basis of the project has no feasible rationality, most obviously because the building is floating. It sort of only belongs to the two states that create that border zone which would be Mexico and the US. It's inhabited essentially by quote/unquote "human capital," which means in the neoliberal policy-scape that it's just a quantity of people. In reality, who they are and what they do isn't really important so much as the fact that they are their own capital. To be in a production setting would be most integral to their own identity. The narrative is extreme in that regard because it completely ignores any human rationality, or any associated humanistic message. Rather, it places them in a strict grid system in which they are funneled as workers throughout it. The main message of the vision was to overillustrate and push forward a message in a kind of future neoliberal world. Humans are only referred to as "human capital" as much as other things are referred to as "oil" or "oil pipelines," "power grids," "telephony," quantities like that.

DV It's a futuristic space for someone to inhabit within the logic of neoliberal rationality. Thus, fictionalization is fundamental.

HB Yeah, if you want to rationalize it based on the research, you would begin in terms of NAFTA or Reagan-era politics in which cooperating countries — Canada, the US and Mexico — would all sort of fall into a terror-free zone, "eliminating" borders, and essentially allowing for the production of goods to be transported duty-free. In this case, we could simply follow other precedents that this would to relate to, such as maquiladoras, which are special economic regions wherein workers are employed along the border and therefore, because of the location of these certain factories, the goods are transported to the US. It's not only cheaper to produce, but things are sold also pretty cheaply as well. If you wanted to rationalize it, I guess the workers would be predicated based off that sort of north/south politics between the US and Mexico. The labor force, depending on wherever future time and space this is, I guess consists of workers filtering into this borderland for immediate capital gain, whether they are US business conglomerates, Mexican factory workers, or US factory workers who go to this frontier zone to be a part of this production system. It paints a very ugly and gray message. I think when this message is pushed to the extreme, the fantastical illustration of it is sort of disgusting. I think the main criteria was not to reduce it to a utopian message but rather to the most dystopian in order to illustrate the precedent behind this fantastical space.

DV I'm curious to know what ideas unfolded after Natalia and Miguel's research on the fictional constructions of the border in relation to language, such as the impossibility of translating that word *frontera*. Or the fact that the border only exists conceptually.

HB Within the fiction of my project, I think about it in relation to a borderless world wherein governments cooperate and produce a sort of economic region in which there is no overarching State that would determine the terms based on who is shipping north and who is shipping south. The main idea was an extra-statecraft world, beyond the State itself. You can create a borderless zone based on its own economic proponents. I think that was the beginning of my vision. Because there is a need to quantify and qualify this zone of mass production, it sort of dissipates the border itself. It benefits both countries equally in this capitalistic society to eliminate all borders. That would only be in terms of movement of goods and human capital, human labor to the extent of people being only used as production means.

You can see that in the precedents of the maquiladoras and the factories along the border, but I also looked into breaking it down a little bit, focusing on oil and gas pipelines, energy networks that are traded between the US and Mexico. Sometimes there will be an energy surplus in Mexico, and that energy gets shipped to cities along the US border, and vice versa. In some ways, it becomes borderless in these specific terms of goods and services exchange, but human capital is eliminated from that equation only so much as to serve the means of production itself. I think the vision plays on the topic of a borderless frontier zone in which capital is the one thing that is strived for and pushed forward, and in doing so disenfranchises those who would actually be in the production zone of this space. In terms of the vision itself, it plays with the idea of a borderless world, but the world is borderless, only to serve those who own the means of production.

I really hope it doesn't reflect on me as an advocate for this super-neoliberal space. Also it's floating, so there's a fantastical layer to the project. Architecture here is sort of thrown out the window, because you don't want to come to terms with the reality of anything that could quantify architecture in source-specific means, for example square footage, certain zoning regions, and things that would control architecture itself. Rather, I looked at policy as a way of creating this. I wasn't only looking at network systems, but switches and resources that can control the space itself. It's a superfuturistic, hypercapitalist zone in which policy is illustrated more fantastically than it is written in sort of black and white script on a page.

DV You want to share any reflections about your experience in this collaborative dynamic in terms of how architecture is imagining the world?

HB For the vision, using architectural representation as a starting base helps produce something more glamorous to look at, while policy has sort of slipped under the rug, even though it really controls the spaces that we inhabit. It's one way of looking at how examining architectural representation can bolster the message of how policy controls this frontier zone.

When I first looked at the black-and-white render drawing, I couldn't possibly imagine the experience of someone being detained at the border, and the legal processes and loopholes that they would inhabit in the following months. At the start I tried to do a rigorous research analysis of where do people go, what people go, where and why and how, and how much it costs, how much time it takes. Thinking in terms of architectural representation itself can help visualize not only for academics to oooh and aaah over, but how this could provide a map for those entering the border.

In the detention centers, how can you begin to imagine the bulging of the wealth associated with the amount of money that is actually filtering into the system? Also, how many people are ignored? How many clerical errors are made that result in people being stuck for months at a time, not being able to apply for asylum because they are immediately deported under certain policy measures? I couldn't possibly imagine that experience. For my own sake, I was using architectural representation in an attempt to illustrate what all those different avenues could look like. That is one part of it, and through a lot of research and going through all the legislation around it, I was really trying to parcel how many people are expeditiously removed. Under Trump there's a policy that's currently expanding, I was curious as to how many people skip out on bond and enter into the population of the US with an insecure legal status. With architectural representation, I think it goes sort of both ways. I can depict a fantastical, heinous landscape and the bluntness of it all. I can also use it to illustrate for those who maybe can't really pick up on paper all of the nuances of legislations. It helps to visualize sort of how many people move through the system.

BEE AWARE

CARLOS ZEDILLO VELASCO

COLUMBUS, OHIO

82.99°

“What distinguishes the worst architect from the best of bees is this, that the architect raises his structure in imagination before he erects it in reality.” Karl Marx establishes this analogy in *Capital*, associating the schematic work of bees but at the same time noting the ability — and responsibility — of architects to design, calculate and anticipate before building.

There are many theories and studies on the connections between species and their natural environment, about environmental degradation and our wasteful consumption of our planet’s natural resources. One of these ideas could help us understand Marx’s metaphor on the relevance of architecture and its habitability and construction. It pertains to a trade that modifies our territory and by doing so, may improve or worsen living conditions in one or several ecosystems. This theory derives from a Kuznets curve, which can be understood as an empirical confirmation of the link between economic growth and environmental degradation as it establishes a correlation between income per capita and environmental decay. In synthesis, Simon Kuznets’s curve theory describes how developing countries must consume and exploit more resources in order to increase their population’s income; once they have achieved this, they will be able to protect their natural environment. Thus, we can assert that developed countries, with income levels higher than the world average, outpace other countries in terms of sustainable development. Denmark, which ranks first in reaching the UN’s Sustainable Development Goals, has achieved 85.2 percent of its goal. In North America, the United States occupies 35th place with 74.5 percent and Mexico 78th place with a 68.5 percent.

At first sight, what this data suggests is that new infrastructure needs to be implemented in developing countries in order to reverse these social disparities, and this implies that the largest architectural projects in the world will happen in countries that are yet to consolidate themselves as solid economies with sustained growth. We must recognize that as we implement these projects, we will somehow modify our territory. This modification must be planned in such a way that

once it has been built it impacts our planet negatively as little as possible.

It is thus more important to reflect on architecture and its possibilities as a form of environmental remediation, not just through certification and the implementation of clean technologies but also in using design as a tool to balance what is being built. For this reason, at Pienza Sostenible we promote the study, analysis, affiliation and implementation of projects that pertain to Mexico's, and the world's, current situation as it relates to the United Nations 2030 Agenda for Sustainable Development, an agreement between government organizations, private entities and citizens.

This includes studying relevant data surrounding each of the 17 Sustainable Development Goals (SDG), as well as organizing expert panels, developing research documents and preparing exhibitions where professionals can respond to specialized information on each goal. Thus we are dedicated to researching the measures and actions that will have a real impact on global sustainability. Furthermore, we develop parametric strategies based on what one country has done in comparison to another.

Mexico, Canada and the United States make up the North American region, a privileged geographical position that allows Mexico to have at its disposal extraordinary economic, social and environmental assets. However, the many kilometers of border Mexico shares with the United States also has great consequences on Mexican territory, heightened by the irresponsible decisions taken by those in power who have not only risked years of joint efforts among nations but have also promoted discrimination and repression between borders.

Far from populist and irresponsible leaderships that have little interest in our environment, terrestrial ecosystems depend on natural pollination to produce the seeds that ensure survival and determine the dynamics of interconnected species. Thus we return to the origin of Marx's analogy. As pollinizing insects, bees favor food diversity, quality and abundance around the world, and provide us with many

products necessary for human life. According to the United Nations Food and Agriculture Organization, 100 crops provide 90 percent of the world's food, and of these 71 are pollinated by bees.

While the United States is third in worldwide honey production, Mexico is sixth and one of the world's leading exporting countries. The states with the highest number of beehives are Jalisco, Chiapas, Campeche, and Yucatán. It is estimated that in the last five years, the number of beehives in the country has decreased by 30 percent. Thus, the volume of Mexico's honey production has dropped 11 percent. There are about 30 thousand bee species in the world and around 25 thousand are effective pollinators. However, they are all vulnerable to intensive agriculture, pesticides, climate change and deficient policies.

Bees are one of the most important living creatures in the world.

The saying that life on Earth would go extinct in four years without the work of productive bees is often attributed to Albert Einstein. Although such affirmation has no scientific basis, there is empirical proof to sustain it. When one analyzes bees individually and as part of a hive, their complexity is clear on many levels: as an organizational structure, in the breeding and development of new bees, in honey production and as a natural environment in apiaries or hives built with specific features. Bees are hard workers, and proof of this is the vast amounts of honey that are produced both in natural and controlled conditions. In this context, and due to the natural conditions in southern and western Mexico, a large volume of honey can be produced and bee protection achieved. Such an enterprise would position our country as one of the main honey producers and exporters in the world — at the same time preserving the biodiversity of our planet's terrestrial ecosystems.

The natural pollination process performed by bees, in unison with other living beings, protects natural diversity and the high nutritional values of the foods we consume, which is

why a decrease in bee population affects us all. At Pienza Sostenible we believe that protecting and caring for bees is a priority we must promote as inhabitants of this planet. As we reflected on this and on how bees can contribute to the world's sustainability, we developed a research project on morphological aspects and issues regarding natural honey production, its subproducts and the flowers that facilitate different types of production.

This project brought together Alberto Kalach, Tatiana Bilbao, Rozana Montiel, Manuel Cervantes and design firm Pirwi — all architects and designers who created a beehive that boosts an increase in bee population and promotes their care and preservation. This project is supported by Betsy de la Vega, who brought to the table her interpretation of handmade textiles produced by Leon XIII Foundation's artisans, thus providing a link between manual work and design requirements. The process has been documented by photographer Fernando Marroquín, who collaborated with the foundation by narrating this story through his lens.

These solutions, beyond the object itself and its architectural program, contribute to our sustainable future over and beyond the environment that was built. It is about providing a perspective that transcends our usual understanding of how we make, relate to and solve architectural projects to make the world a better place. On this basis we have been able to prove that despite politics, threats and treaties, walls cannot divide countries whose hybridization has bred ideas that have been catalyzed and potentialized on both sides of the border.

UNION, OHIO

IWAN BAAN

84.30°

UNION, OHIO

84.30°

UNION, OHIO

84.30°

UNION, OHIO

UNION, OHIO

84.30°

UNION, OHIO

84.30°

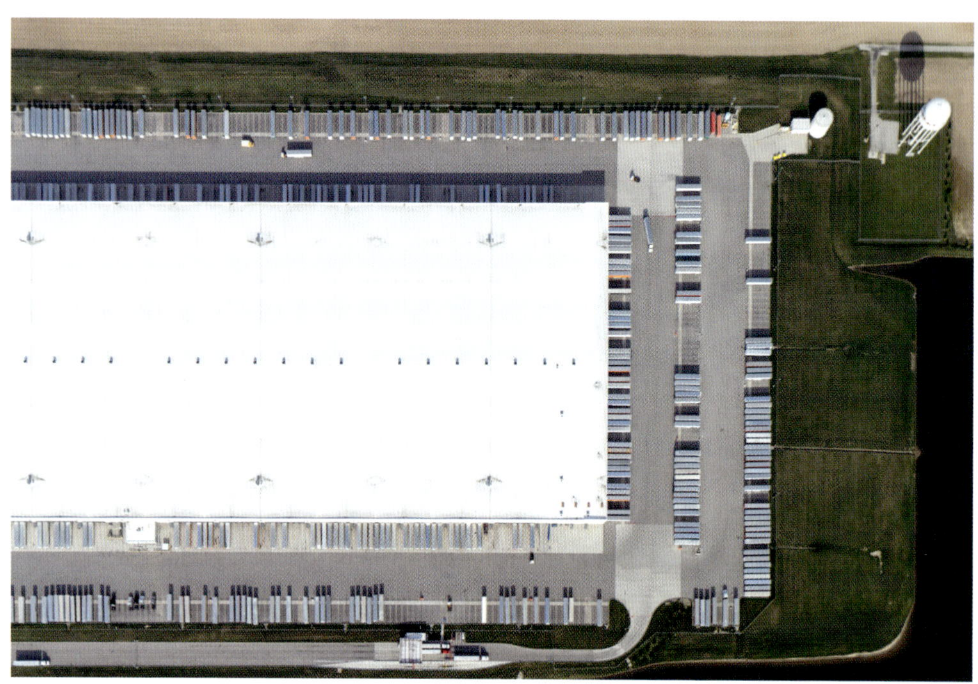

UNION, OHIO

84.30°

UNION, OHIO

84.30°

IMAGINING THE FRONTIER CARLOS HAGERMAN

DZONCAUICH, YUCATÁN 88.89°

It is curious how the notion of the frontier evokes different interpretations in the collective imagination. That line clearly marked on a map, often in a different color, borders and delimits two territories. Off the map and back in the real world, the frontier is sometimes invisible and sometimes marked by striking economic and social differences etched on the landscape. But the frontier is more powerful than either a map or a landscape. It is a concept that exists in the way we think, the way we feel, in the way we imagine the other side.

For twelve years I have been investigating the imaginaries of the Mexico–United States frontier through my profession as a filmmaker. These are the different windows I have opened up on the theme.

Those Who Remain / Los que se quedan

In 2006 I had the opportunity to make a documentary film, together with Juan Carlos Rulfo, about the lives of Mexican families who had a member living in the United States as a migrant. Families that for years lived without a father, a brother, a daughter, a husband. The aim was to present a wide range of stories that might reveal the emotional cost of migration. We called it *Those Who Remain.*

Leaving behind academic debates, statistics and hard data, we explored the relationships between men, women, boys and girls with real names. In each case, "the frontier" was a symbol of something different.

The film begins with a prologue where in a classroom the kindergarten teacher asks: Who wants to go to the United States? All the boys and girls respond in unison "Meeeee!" raising their hands excitedly. They are children just four or five years old, yet already have this dream of what is on the other side of the frontier.

When the teacher asks why they want to go, a boy answers "because there's money lying around on the ground," and a girl says "because there's gifts and gold chains." The notion is already implanted in their imagination that the place on the other side of the frontier is like Ali Baba's cave where all the treasure is just waiting to be gathered.

We filmed in six different regions across Mexico and in each one we visited a school; sometimes elementary schools, sometimes junior or senior high schools. We always asked the teacher to put the same question to the students: "Who wants to go to the United States?" We always saw the same pattern of answers. It was extraordinary to observe this dream of abundance as a cultural phenomenon that permeates from Yucatán to Zacatecas, from the age of four to sixteen. Of all the classrooms we filmed in, we chose the one with the youngest children to start the film, because they are the ones who reproduce unfiltered what they see and hear, their culture at home. Their concept of the frontier is naïve, but even though it may seem absurd to think that there is "money lying around on the ground" the idea is not so distant from the illusion that it is easy to get over "there" in order to solve the problem of "here."

One of the stories in the film is that of Maricela and her four children, in which we observe as they prepare to say goodbye to their village in Yucatán and set off on a journey to meet up with the father in

Los Angeles. Here, the frontier is an obstacle that has to be ovecome. There is a great deal of complexity in this family. When we met Maricela, the first thing she told us is that she didn't want to cross over: "If my husband wants to be with his family, then he should come back." Many in her village wanted her to put herself forward as candidate for mayor, and she was also organizing weekly meetings for women whose husbands were in the United States. We thought this was a good story to tell: that of a woman who wanted to stay. But as often happens in documentaries, people's lives change and the story ended up being one of a family that left.

Maricela had no illusions about what life was like over there; she knew perfectly well. As a young woman she had gone to the United States and that's where she had met Ángel, her husband. She had already crossed via the desert and knew the dangers it involved. Even so, she had the hope of becoming a complete family again, of no longer missing the embrace of her partner and her children growing up with their father present. By contrast, for her daughters, the US was the place where they were going to discover what theme parks are. In the middle of the film, the oldest daughter, Evelyn, writes a letter to her father imagining what those parks look like and how she sees her family all enjoying them.

To contrast the experience of the dream of family reunification, the documentary also tells the story of Don

Pascual and Doña Juanita, a pair of older peasant farmers who haven't seen their children for eight years. All these years they have cultivated the field of garlic that Marcos, their oldest son, left them before he left. Neither Pascual nor Juanita have even crossed the frontier of their own state; for them the "over there" where their children live is a mystery from which money sometimes arrives to build a house little by little. The promise is that once the house is finished, their children will come back to live in it.

Another story is that of Yaremi, a fourteen-year-old teenager who had made a commitment to study as hard as she could, but with a sense of guilt because her father left to work in the US for seven years so that she and her sisters could keep studying. In the film, Yaremi's mother recounts how her daughter told her father by telephone that "even if it means we only have an avocado to eat, I want you to come back."

At the time we were filming, Yaremi's father, Rodolfo, had just returned, to find his daughter all grown-up and not the seven-year-old girl he'd left behind. Neither of the two knew how to deal with a relationship with someone who they didn't really know any longer. The frontier represents the impossibility of having been together at the most important moments of their lives. The frontier is an abyss, a void that is impossible to fill in.

There was a moment when we thought that the ideal end to the documentary

would be a helicopter shot, a long shot flying over the Pacific with the camera very close to the water, where there is no line to mark the frontier, nor even any differences in the landscape. Only water, the water of the sea. And then, abruptly, posts rise out of the water, defining the difference between the territories. The posts grow taller and taller until they form a fence, a barrier that reaches the shore, and then a wall that determines the physical division of the two territories until reaching the watchtower.

The relevant permits were requested from both countries and the scene was filmed. The most expensive scene of the movie. But in the end, we decided to cut it. In the context of the film, it was an impersonal and conceptual scene, impressive to see, but one that distracted from our intention to focus on the outcomes of the characters whose life stories we had been exploring.

All of us who participated in the film were deeply moved by the stories of these families. *Those Who Remain* led us to never see our country the same way again.

Back to Life / Vuelve a la Vida

To speak of both sides of the frontier, we have to take into account the migratory movement that also happens from north to south. Who are the Americans who migrate to Mexico in search of a better life? What does a better life mean for them? What are their priorities?

In 2005 I had the good fortune to learn about the love story between Robyn Sidney, a dazzling red-haired top model from New York, and Hilario Martínez Valdivia, better known as "El Perro Largo," a legendary diver from Acapulco. In the 1960s, after meeting Hilario, Robyn decided to abandon her modeling career and migrate to Mexico with John, the young, freckled son from her first marriage, seeking tranquillity, the warmth of the sea and of the people of Acapulco. Seeking to come back to life.

With this crossing to the other side, this time from north to south, we encounter three different ideas of the frontier. The first idea Is Robyn's: the frontier

as freedom. The possibility to change your life. To start over. The freedom to swap some things for others: the camera flashes for moonlit nights on the beach, the life among jazz musicians and Manhattan intellectuals for boleros with family and friends on Caleta Beach, the subway and the skyscraper canyons for swimming with manta rays in the Boca Chica coral reef. All this dream of "romantic Mexico," just like the "American dream" pursued by the migrants who travel in the opposite direction, is also a mirage.

The second vision of the frontier is that of El Perro Largo. The diver who caught the American tourist and made her his wife. The couple who educate their children aware of a very particular cultural mixture. For Perro Largo the frontier is one of understanding, reflected in how he introduces his wife into a social life that is more of the common people where Robyn's height stood out all over. And also reflected in his tireless effort to teach Robyn the sound of the rolled "r" in Spanish, making her sing to the point of exhaustion the words "r con r cigarro, r con r barril, rápido ruedan los carros cargados de azúcar del ferrocarril."

The third vision of the frontier is the most complex of all. This is the perspective of John. As a child he was never asked if he wanted to live in Mexico, if he was happy to come to a place where he didn't speak the language, of studying in a school where his fellow students called

him "gringo caga leche" because he was the only freckled, pale-skinned boy in the public primary school in the center of Acapulco. John told us about this in an interview for *Back to Life*, "with the sun, my freckles got bigger, they were horrible . . . once a friend told me to use donkey dung . . . his sister had a mark on her skin and it went with donkey dung." For John, the frontier was a huge unknown that he bore on his shoulders; he was different, he was the one who didn't belong. So what was he doing in Acapulco?

The character of John appears in two situations over the course of the documentary. First, as a child growing up eating ice lollies on the beach, and second as an adult living back in the United States with his own family. He lived in Acapulco for 18 years, and at the time of shooting the film he'd been living back in Los Angeles for 18 years. The frontier had changed its meaning already twice in his life. The first wasn't his decision, but the second was. He explains this as he drives along the freeway in Los Angeles: "the difficult thing is that on the outside I'm a gringo, tall, freckles and green eyes, but on the inside I'm a Mexican." The frontier, which was such a visible contrast as a child, is now invisible but just as confusing. Before the end of the film, John will decide once again to change and this time to take his whole family back to Mexico; now his own children will be the

ones to experience the decision to migrate taken by their father.

The enormous difference with this inverted mirror is that here the frontier is a choice. John can come and go when he chooses. Robyn chose to leave behind her life in New York, but always had the freedom to return. After forty years of living a block from Caleta Beach, Robyn asserts, with shining eyes and with a strong American accent: "you are from where you live, not from where you're born."

Invisible Children

I am currently developing a documentary with Brinca animation studio on the stories of children and young adults who live in the United States from undocumented families. The film is based on testimonies about what it is like to live with the vulnerability that any day your parents can be arrested and deported. Here the frontier lies in the past, in the moment when these mothers and fathers decide to cross over to try to offer their children better possibilities.

This is a documentary animation film, which means we are using real testimonies and added the storytelling tools of animation. There are two reasons for this. The first is to preserve the anonymity of the families. The second is that an animation allows you to create visual metaphors to tell stories and memories from the past, like the dreams of hope and fears of the future from a completely subjective viewpoint.

Generally, these children and young adults are not very rooted in the culture of their parents. This is partly because of the impossibility of legally crossing the border to discover their roots. But also because the parents, as a defense mechanism, encourage them to integrate and form part of American society, forgetting their own background. This creates a new vision of the frontier; this time looking from the United States toward Mexico. They receive an idyllic version full of stories of what their village was like, the grandparents, the landscape and the fields.

One of the stories in this new documentary is that of Evelyn and Elizabeth, who I met during the filming of *Those Who Remain*. Evelyn is the daughter of Maricela and Ángel, who as mentioned before met in the United States. Evelyn was born there and as a young girl returned with her parents to Dzoncauich, Yucatán, the birthplace of Maricela. There they had three further children: Elizabeth, Effy and Angelito. Some years later, the paternal grandmother of the children fell ill in Los Angeles and Ángel decided to go and see her. He then stayed there, until Maricela decided to cross the border with all the children. At the end of the film *Those Who Remain*, we see them go from house to house saying farewell, embracing and weeping with their friends and relatives.

What we don't see in the film is how they did the border. Evelyn crossed first, with her US passport, while her three

siblings had to do it on different trips using fake papers. Maricela crossed through the desert and almost lost her life. Today, ten years after *Those Who Remain*, we took up the story again from the perspective of the children to recount what happened since they crossed and how they feel now.

Evelyn is twenty-two years old, and as the oldest daughter, with US nationality, she bears on her shoulders the dream that through her the rest of her family will be able to obtain papers. In addition, she carries the pressure of securing a successful financial future in order to get her family out of the huge difficulties they face as undocumented migrants. For Evelyn, the frontier weighs on her.

Elizabeth is twenty years old and finished senior high school. She is the best friend of her sister but feels that her future opportunities are cut short by her migratory status. She can't continue her studies and she's finding it very hard to find a job as she needs a fake Social Security number. Her dream is to run a bakery, but without papers she can't own a business. Nor is the answer to return to Mexico: she has grown up in the United States, she is more comfortable speaking English than Spanish, she doesn't want to be separated from her family and cannot imagine going to live in a Yucatán village. Her view of the future is very bleak and the American dream seems unreachable. For Elizabeth, the frontier is a double impossibility.

My Frontier

Making these films has allowed me to hear hundreds of hours of stories from women, men and children about how it feels to be far from home, whether missing someone they love or growing up in a culture that is not their own, but end up appropriating it however they can. The phenomenon of migration implies the most important exchange of ideas between Mexico and the United States. Cultures mix and create new subcultures that blend differences with similarities. In this way, no matter whether taller and stronger walls are built, people will always be curious to know about what is happening on the other side.

The frontier is and always will be an imaginary full of stories.

MUKSEOGA MINJAE KIM

MÉRIDA, YUCATÁN 89.59°

April 4, 1905, *Il Ford*, a British cargo ship, set out on a six-week-long journey from Jaemulpo, an international port of the Chosun Empire. The Chosun Empire was in its dwindling state, only seven months away from signing its rights off to the Empire of Japan. Aboard the ship along with the crew were 1,033 Koreans; farmers, laborers, aristocrats and some 200 retired soldiers; all eager to find a new life elsewhere. Their destination was called Mukseoga, "a civilized powerhouse neighboring the United States where rich soils and warm weather prevented diseases, and the bountiful wealth made laborers scarce."

This brief description of Mukseoga was found in an immigration advertisement in newspapers, recruiting for imported labor. It was truly a lucrative offer. A four-year contract guaranteed a fortune big enough to acquire land in Korea, on top of generous benefits such as child support, education and medical care. Applicants were even encouraged to move with their family as it provided stability to the workers. The Chosun Empire was getting taken over by the Empire of Japan and would only exist as a colony by 1906. The military was shut down, and people were losing faith in the stability of their nation. Nobody had heard of Mukseoga before, but it was an option, nonetheless.

In the newspaper which used both hangul (Korean alphabet) and Chinese characters, Mukseoga was spelled "墨西哥." As Chinese characters are ideograms, the three letters vaguely translate to "the song of the dark west." Although this might have left an impression, it actually carried no true meaning, as Mukseoga was a transliterated title. Since Korean culture and Chinese culture shared Chinese characters as written language but had distinctively different spoken languages, 墨西哥 read as [mukseoga] in Korea while it read as [Mòxīgē] in China, which sounds much closer to the actual destination of the *Il Ford*: Mexico.

The *Il Ford* was off to Salina Cruz on the western coast of Mexico. The 1,033 Koreans would then board a train to cross the narrow land between the two coasts, only to take another ship on the Atlantic Ocean which eventually brought them to Port Progreso on the Yucatán peninsula. Their long journey ended in Mérida, 35 km south from Progreso, when they were sold off to 25 different haciendas around the region as slave labor.

There must have been a delirious moment when the Koreans realized that they were in fact in Mexico. Mexico was a rather different place from Mukseoga. The tropical climate of Yucatán peninsula was insufferable to the Koreans. Poverty and corruption was so prevalent under the iron-fisted rule of Porfirio Díaz that the nation was boiling over into a revolution. They operated under a peonage system which had enslaved a majority of the native Mayans. The laborers at haciendas were confined within the property and were subject to an internal economy. They were paid with wooden notes to be used as currency to buy groceries and daily necessities at inflated prices from in-house stores, designed to indenture workers as they accumulated debt.

The main crop harvested at the haciendas were henequen plants. This agave plant, native to the region, was the golden industry of the era. The fiber harvested from the leaves were used to make marine-grade ropes, which were in high demand due to competitive global expeditions in search of new colonies. The leaves were as tall as a grown man and the thorns it grew on its blades would cut into the hands of the workers. Each worker was required to harvest thousands of leaves a day, and quite often, their wives and children would join them at the field to meet the

quota. There were no facilities for children, so often they had to be brought out to the field and left in the shade of a tree.

Some of the Korean immigrants had tried to reach home to extricate themselves from slavery, but what was sent back was only the devastating news that Korea had been taken over by Japan. 1,033 Koreans, scattered across Yucatán peninsula, were the only Korean bodies adrift in the all of Latin America, and there was no Korea for them to go back to. Over the years, most of the Koreans were able to pay off their debt at the haciendas and gain freedom. But rather than going back to occupied Korea, they chose to stay in Mexico. It wasn't until 1945, 40 years after the departure from Jaemulpo, when they were finally able to celebrate Korea's independence from Japan, yet only to be heartbroken in 1950 by the news of the Korean war, completely discouraging the Koreans who were opening up to the idea of visiting home. Until the 1960s, when South Korea formally established diplomatic relations with Mexico, there was no subsequent emigration to Mexico from Korea.

Through the decades that came after 1905 are speckles of amalgamations of Korea and Mexico: Last names such as Ko, Choi, or Hwang became Corona, Sanchez, or Juárez. *Henequen* became a slang referring to Koreans. There used to be a bar called Jaemulpo in Mérida in honor of the patrons who would drunkenly cry out the port that became the last sight of the motherland. Within the revolutionary army that fought for Villa, Zapata and Obregón were mercenaries who were trained to fight for the Korean king. Some even participated in the revolutions in Cuba and Guatemala. Álvaro Obregón, postrevolution president of Mexico from 1920 to 1924, had a Korean barber.

To reflect on these moments, it is interesting to think that the destination of 1,033 Koreans was Mukseoga, not Mexico. There was no way for the Koreans to have an experience of Mexico that is not obscured by their Korean heritage or culture and Mexico couldn't reflect the Koreans without projecting its own history as well. After all, there is probably some truth to it if one was to argue that the 1,033 Koreans did live in Mukseoga: a transliterated Korean experience of Mexico. Somehow the aspiration, excitement and fear of departing, and the nostalgia, agony and anger of the emigrated are captured in the essence of Mukseoga. It was a destination that they could never reach, yet also a limbo that they could never escape from.

A. Due to the Confucian values, nineteenth-century Korea was a society that strictly practiced separation among classes and genders. Extensive social practices and regulations accumulated over centuries ensured the stability of the division although at the turn of the century, this began to crumble as the nation was at the verge of its collapse. The Korean population on the *Il Ford* faced a unique challenge of being deprived of any spatial practice that allowed for separation and was forced to integrate across class and gender.

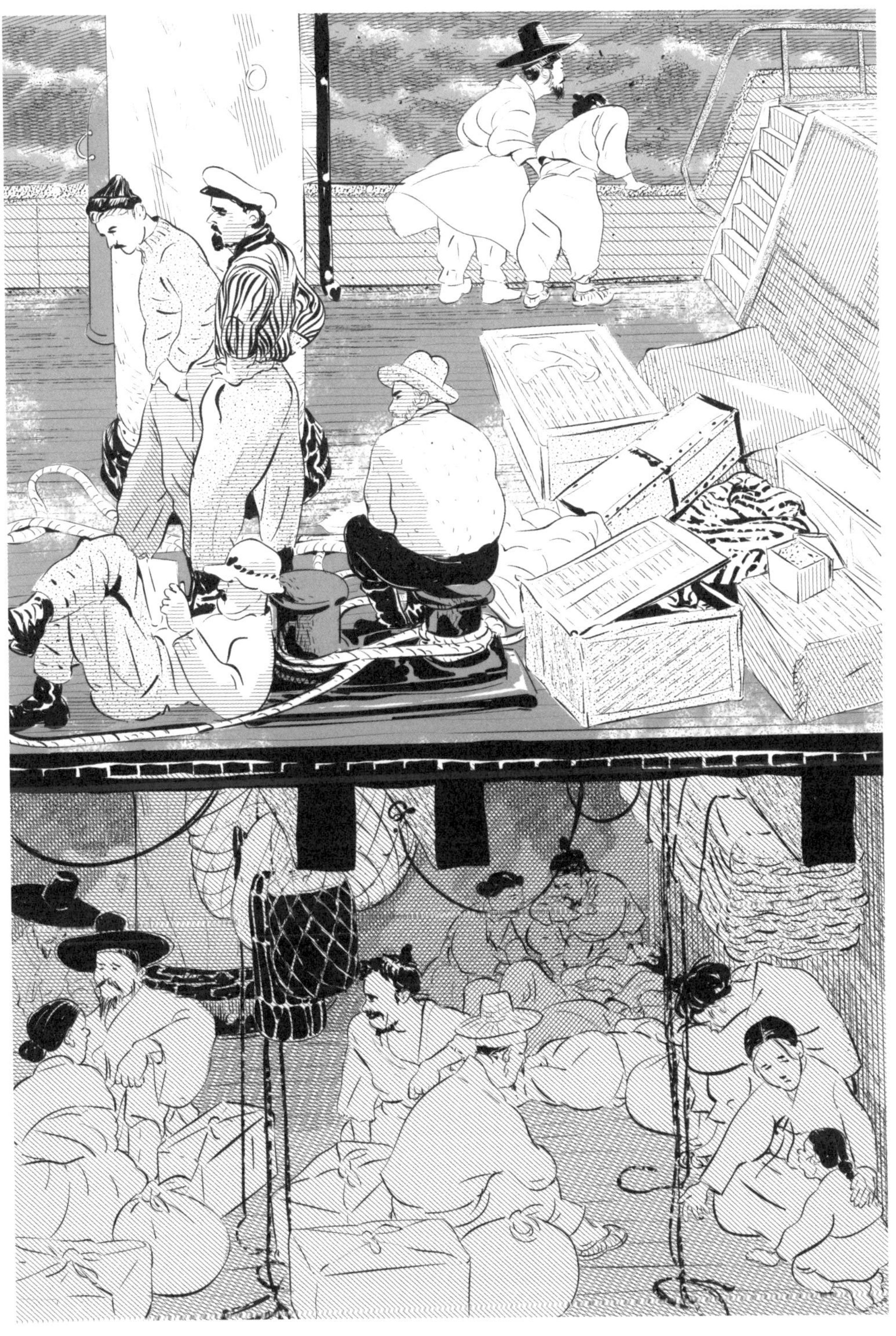

B. Most of the Koreans who were sent to the haciendas in Yucatán were housed along with working indigenous Mayans in Mayan huts called Na or Paja. These thatched dwellings were not so different from traditional Korean huts with straw roofs and mudded walls between wooden posts. While Mayan huts provided singular space that allowed cooking on dirt floor, and sleeping on elevated hammocks, suspended across the structure, Koreans often built a separate kitchen outside for cooking, and padded the interior floor with straw mats to accommodate living and sleeping on the floor.

Integration with Mayan culture came naturally as the Koreans worked and lived together with the Mayans. Since there was an imbalance in gender among the group of Koreans, intercultural marriage between Korean men and Mayan women was quite frequent. As polygamy was quite common in Korea, some Korean men would take a Mayan woman as a second wife.

Depicted in this drawing is a Korean household in their domestic environment. While a family including a Mayan woman is preparing kimchi with nopal, a common edible cactus in Mexico, another woman is working on protective gear such as gloves and shin guards worn while harvesting henequens.

C. After leaving the haciendas, the Koreans participated in various trades to make a living and moved across Latin America, notably to Havana and Mexico City in search for new opportunities. As they spread, they still kept the Korean communities very organized, often mobilized enough to send their savings to activists fighting for Korean independence back home.

Kim Ikju was one of the community leaders who organized these efforts in Mexico City and Tampico. The drawing shows a Korean building he built in Tampico which became a local attraction. The building stood for decades until it was lost during a storm season.

D. At the turn of the century there was a series of military reforms in the Chosun Empire in attempts to modernize itself until eventually the entire Korean military was decommissioned in 1907. The reforms caused an overflow of retired soldiers around the nation which explains how the one-fifth of the 1,033 Koreans aboard *Il Ford* were military veterans.

They played a pivotal role in organizing communities in the posthacienda days. When the haciendas began releasing the Koreans, led by a few veterans, the Korean community instituted daily military training that eventually formalized as a military school in Mérida in order to empower themselves and eventually defeat the Japanese occupation in Korea.

In 1909, on the fourth anniversary of Japanese takeover, the Korean community organized a military march in downtown Mérida with the entire city and the governor of Yucatán as the audience claiming the illegitimacy of Japan's seizure: 110 men and women marched with Korean and Mexican flags, singing the Korean anthem, proclaiming their voice and identity to the general public in Mexico for the first time. The celebration of this event lasted a couple of days and included a mock-battle between two parties each dressed up as Korean and Japanese military. More than 10,000 km away from the Korean peninsula, was a scenario where Korea was not defeated by Japan.

When the revolution swept Mexico, many of the Korean veterans participated, aiding whichever side they could join. As aged veterans, some even participated in the Cuban and Guatemalan revolutions. The revolutionary force in Guatemala had promised a plot of land and money for participating Koreans but after a few casualties the Koreans retreated, afraid of losing members of their already diminutive community.

AUSTIN, TEXAS
PUEBLA CITY, PUEBLA
McALLEN, TEXAS/REYNOSA, TAMAULIPAS
MEXICO CITY, CIUDAD DE MÉXICO
MONTERREY, NUEVO LEÓN
ACÁMBARO, GUANAJUATO
ULYSSES, KANSAS

IWAN BAAN

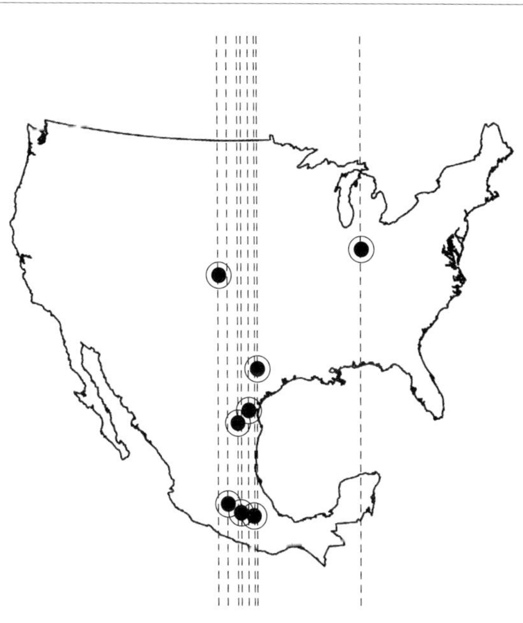

97.74°, 98.20°, 98.23°, 99.13°, 100.31°, 100.71°, 101.35°

AUSTIN, TEXAS

AUSTIN, TEXAS

ATM
PUBLIC
PARKING
P3018
PREMIUM
PARKING
ATM

AUSTIN, TEXAS

AUSTIN, TEXAS

AUSTIN, TEXAS

JESSUS IS Coming
Soon
Breakfast Tacos

AUSTIN, TEXAS

AUSTIN, TEXAS

SAN JOSE

AUSTIN, TEXAS

2018
NDEROS PARTY OF TWO

PUEBLA CITY, PUEBLA

98.20°

PUEBLA CITY, PUEBLA

PUEBLA CITY, PUEBLA

98.20°

PUEBLA CITY, PUEBLA

98.20°

PUEBLA CITY, PUEBLA

98.20°

PUEBLA CITY, PUEBLA

PUEBLA CITY, PUEBLA

PUEBLA CITY, PUEBLA

PUEBLA CITY, PUEBLA

98.20°

McALLEN, TEXAS / REYNOSA, TAMAULIPAS

98.23°

McALLEN, TEXAS / REYNOSA, TAMAULIPAS

...just be nice.

McALLEN, TEXAS / REYNOSA, TAMAULIPAS

98.23°

McALLEN, TEXAS / REYNOSA, TAMAULIPAS

98.23°

McALLEN, TEXAS / REYNOSA, TAMAULIPAS

98.23°

McALLEN, TEXAS / REYNOSA, TAMAULIPAS

98.23°

McALLEN, TEXAS / REYNOSA, TAMAULIPAS

98.23°

MEXICO CITY, CIUDAD DE MÉXICO

MEXICO CITY, CIUDAD DE MÉXICO

MEXICO CITY, CIUDAD DE MÉXICO

MEXICO CITY, CIUDAD DE MÉXICO

MONTERREY, NUEVO LEÓN

100.31°

MONTERREY, NUEVO LEÓN

100.31°

MONTERREY, NUEVO LEÓN

Semillero Purísima.
Vive en

MONTERREY, NUEVO LEÓN

MONTERREY, NUEVO LEÓN

100.31°

ACÁMBARO, GUANAJUATO

120
CORONEO
120
JERECUARO
120
NUEVO CHUPICUARO

ACÁMBARO, GUANAJUATO

100.71°

ACÁMBARO, GUANAJUATO

100.71°

ACÁMBARO, GUANAJUATO

100.71°

ACÁMBARO, GUANAJUATO

ULYSSES, KANSAS

101.35°

ULYSSES, KANSAS

101.35°

ULYSSES, KANSAS

101.35°

ULYSSES, KANSAS

20

ULYSSES, KANSAS

101.35°

ULYSSES, KANSAS

101.35°

ULYSSES, KANSAS

BAKERY
KITCHEN RULES
★ No Complaining

ULYSSES, KANSAS

eam Shop
eteria
eteria
y
everia
uhtemoc
356-2290
211
GRANT COUNTY
MEDICAL EQUIPMENT LLC
356-1373
Home Oxygen & Respiratory Care

101.35°

ULYSSES, KANSAS

101.35°

ULYSSES, KANSAS

101.35°

THE MIGRATION OF MONEY, OBJECTS AND ASPIRATIONS: A 100-YEAR-LONG REGIONAL HISTORY

SARAH LYNN LOPEZ

GUADALAJARA, JALISCO

103.34°

The movement of money, things and materials is about relationships between people. Friendships, kinships, links to places and a search for meaning motivate people to create robust social and spatial networks that endure generations and span great distances. Between Mexico and the United States, the crisscrossing of objects, dollars and aspirations is motivated by individuals who lead transborder lives.

If we start in 1848 with the delineation of what has evolved into the US–Mexico boundary, there have been 171 years of engagement between disparate places that can be traced and tracked in things, architectures, archives and oral histories. These networks operate regionally; social and economic geographies are created by people operating from a specific set of places in Mexico to specific places in the US. A messy set of overlapping and intersecting points of connection that cover the Southwest and northern Mexico extend outward into the interior of both nations. From the point of view of this interconnected region it is sometimes hard to see distinct nation-states.

In the 1920s and 1930s, anthropologist Manuel Gamio and political economist Paul S. Taylor were both commissioned by the Social Science Research Council to study the "Mexican problem," or the impact of mass migration from Mexico to US farms on Mexican and American society.[1] In the first several decades of the twentieth century, individuals who went to the US were recorded as earning from between five to thirty-six times what they could earn in Mexican towns. These ratios were dramatically higher for rural workers, who earned far less in Mexico than townspeople did. Taylor and Gamio note that the tremendous imbalance created by enormous wage differentials alone would have sufficed to cause heavy emigration.[2] Political, environmental and economic conditions — including the Mexican Revolution (ca. 1910–20), the Cristero War (1926–29), drought and new railroads — produced structural conditions that further supported emigration.

Forerunners in what is now framed as transnational, transborder and/or translocal research, Manuel Gamio's team interviewed migrants living in different US cities to better understand their social and cultural "adaptation and resistance" to American ways of life. Researchers also visited migrant hometowns in Mexico to photograph the influence of migration on place.[3] Taylor, interested in Mexican hometown societal transformations due to migration, went to live in Arandas, Jalisco, for several months, documenting an emergent clash between provincial agrarian livelihoods and lessons learned in the industrial North. Taylor's report, *A Spanish-Mexican Peasant Community: Arandas in Jalisco, Mexico*, presents a portrait of Mexican modernity in the 1930s.[4] Through their research, archival material, such as draft transfers sent from California banks to Mexican towns, are contextualized in broader social, spatial and material change. According to the *New York Times,* in 1928 Mexico received twelve million dollars in remittances.[5]

The specifics of transborder material transformation are captured in the Department of Foreign Relations' customs forms and research field notes describing and photographing individual preferences and attire.[6] Taylor records migrants' penchant for buying wristwatches, overalls, and sewing machines.[7] These objects had different symbolic meanings and each affected daily life differently. The wristwatch introduced an American idea of time and timeliness to rural towns where people worked with the sun and where church bells structured daily routines. Overalls became a ubiquitous form of dress. According to Taylor, it was "obvious that the migrant standard and kind of dress became a factor in setting new standards for nonemigrants who could afford it."[8] Introducing overalls marks a broader cultural moment when foreign dress began to redefine local standards.[9] The introduction of the sewing machine created a great divide between women who used them and those who sewed by hand. This did not end sewing by hand in the pueblo; rather, it created new comparisons and relative satisfactions for those who sewed by hand and those who did not (have to). These imports also signified migrants' contributions to the uneven economic development of families and communities.

While clothing and durable goods differentiated community members along nascent class lines, the introduction of imported automobiles produced more comprehensive spatial change in rural Mexico.[10] Gamio records that one out of every three migrants in his study brought a car back with him or her to Mexico. A record of custom-free objects brought from the US into Mexico in 1927 documents eighteen different car manufactures including Chevrolet, Studebaker and Pontiac.[11] This influx of automobiles led to the construction of roads:

> The possession of automobiles is absolutely unheard of in the humble social class to which the immigrants generally belong. . . . Many sections of rural Mexico where the repatriated immigrant goes to colonize have no suitable automobile roads, and either there is no gasoline or else it is expensive or hard to get, with the result that automobiles are often useless. The good that results is that the possession of automobiles stimulates the owners to build roads, however poor these might be due to the humble circumstances of the owners. It would have been better had they brought in more buggies and carriages.[12]

The extent to which repatriated migrants actually built new roads is unknown. This quotation, however, is evidence that the newly acquired modern amenity — the car — caused migrants to perceive a deficiency in their built environment that they attempted to correct through collective action. This makes road building a social process and indicates that financing roads with remitted dollars was one of the initial built environment changes in rural communities linked to remittances. This view is supported by the fact that fewer than one-third of imported vehicles were trucks suited to rough roads and heavy work; over two-thirds were passenger cars. In a series of migrant portraits taken by Gamio in Michoacán,

1. Recently returning from the US, Mexican migrants pose in front of a remitted Ford automobile in Mexico, photographed by Manuel Gamio's research team in 1937. Courtesy of the Bancroft Library at the University of California, Berkeley.

Mexico, repatriated migrants posed in their US "Sunday best" in front of a model-T Ford. The same car was used in all of the portraits, providing a photogenic symbol of American modernity as migrant success.[13] [Figure 1]

Despite the introduction of dollars and cars, major spatial change did not appear to have taken hold of rural localities and small towns during the period of Gamio's and Taylor's studies. Some migrants were interested in building a home in the "American style," but this desire was quickly set aside by the logistical and practical difficulties of doing so. In Arandas, Taylor records a return migrant's musings regarding a new home: "I would like to have a house in American style. . . . But . . . here we build thick so no bullet can come through, and no windows, so when the door is shut, no one can come."[14] Migrants who did build American-style houses quickly reverted back to their old customs and sought refuge in traditional-style homes. A local nonmigrant in Arandas told Taylor: "When the Mexicans come from the United States they are converted. They have better manners, dress and more money. They learn to wash their faces. . . . Many live in a *jacal* [traditional house], and upon return, make a new house. . . . But after [a *norteño*] has been here for a time, he loses his learning and his wishes and makes his living as before."[15]

From the perspective of some nonmigrant inhabitants in Arandas, migrants were perceived as a threat to patriotism. Taylor records the voice of a leading merchant in Arandas: "Every Mexican who goes, likes the United States better than Mexico. He gets a better life there than here. After 100 years, it will be good-bye to Mexico. I am afraid they will like America better than Mexico. We are making 'war' so they won't become Americanized. They will not like the Mexican flag; they have no love of country, and that is a great danger to Mexico."[16]

While this merchant is certain that migrants "like America better than Mexico," Taylor argues that migrants were actually ambivalent regarding their preference of country: "But with a large proportion of the returned emigrants, the happier life in Mexico was more than counterbalanced by the higher material

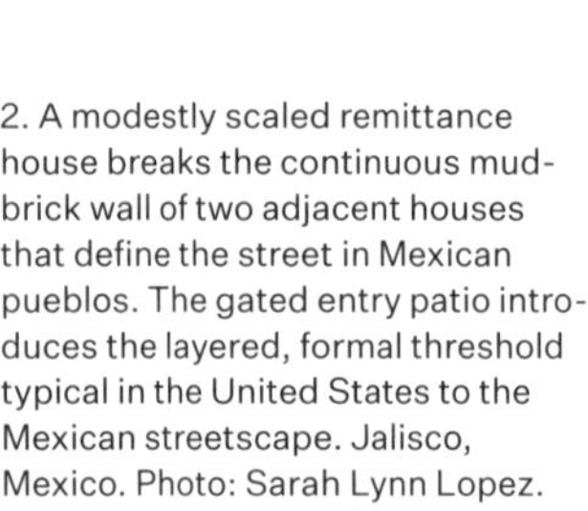

2. A modestly scaled remittance house breaks the continuous mud-brick wall of two adjacent houses that define the street in Mexican pueblos. The gated entry patio introduces the layered, formal threshold typical in the United States to the Mexican streetscape. Jalisco, Mexico. Photo: Sarah Lynn Lopez.

3. A cognitive map of San Juan de Amula, based on one woman's knowledge about the sources of funding used to build locals' homes — remittances sent by migrants, remittances combined with pesos, or only pesos. Jalisco, Mexico. Drawing: Chesney Floyd.

standard of living in the United States. Many asserted that they were happier in Arandas, and almost in the next breath, that they would go back to the United States if work was plentiful, and would gladly live there the remainder of their lives, apparently seeing no contradiction in their statements."[17] While Taylor was researching migrant housing conditions in California, he approached a couple living in a self-built shack under a tree and asked the owners why they did not invest more in their housing. They replied that they did not know if they would stay and that they might return to Mexico. He then asked, "How long have you been here?" to which they responded, "Thirty years."[18] Taylor notes: "Since it [Mexico] was immediately adjacent geographically, it was also close psychologically in the minds of Mexican immigrants in the United States."[19]

The modest changes in Mexico's built environment recorded by Gamio and Taylor in the 1920s and 30s have today exploded into a full-scale transformation of the architecture and landscape of so-called rural towns due, in part, to what I call "the remittance house."[20] Inspired by Gamio and Taylor's work, since 2004 I have expanded upon their geographic base to document remittance houses in Jalisco, Guanajuato, Michoacán, San Luis Potosí, Yucatán, and Oaxaca. New houses in Mexico financed by dollars earned in the US warrant the term *remittance house* because their material aspects (the building's bones, shell, architectural plan and siting) are inseparable from the social spaces that animate them, social spaces that are increasingly defined by *remitting as a way of life*. The social spheres of migrants who are working in the US while maintaining active ties to childhood towns and managing families dispersed across geographies, are social spheres increasingly structured by the logic of remittance. In this migratory space, distance is normalized and incorporated into a way of life that manages separation, dispersion, fragmentation and ambivalence on a daily basis.

Remittance homes tend to disrupt small-town fabrics: new houses are pulled back from the continuous facade, second

4. Two local businesses are influenced by their owners' migration histories: a two-story house converted into a US-style car wash called Beverly Hills Autobaño and the convenience store El 7 Eleven on the side of the road. Jalisco, Mexico. Photos: Sarah Lynn Lopez.

5. A "typical Mexican courtyard" in a migrant-owned urban house in Bell, California, displays an imported *cantera* stone fountain, hand-carved in Mexico. Photo: Sarah Lynn Lopez.

stories emerge, houses are brightly colored and hyper-ornamental. An architecture of facades emerges as migrants attempt to distinguish themselves from those who have never left the village. Details such as classically styled columns reinterpreting the volumes and ornamental carving of Ionic and Corinthian orders allow home owners and builders to represent a diverse set of experiences. Mexican craftsmanship is combined with "*estilo Californiano*" recessed yards, metal fences, carports and picture windows.[21] These homes transform streetscapes, blocks, neighborhoods and entire towns. A cognitive map drawn by a resident of San Juan de Amula, a 400-person pueblo, illustrates the endemic and ever-present spread of the remittance house in her town. [Figures 2 and 3]

It is not only the remittance house that is transforming the Mexican built environment. Entire *remittance landscapes* are produced from continuous movement between Mexico and the US.[22] Migrants who have spent varying amounts of time in the US are returning to Mexico to open businesses modeled off of their experiences abroad. "El 7 Eleven" stands in as a substitute for the global franchise, which is not common in the south of Jalisco. Car washes are a microindustry in rural localities often financed and managed by return emigrants. The owner of the Beverly Hills Autobaño in Los Altos de Jalisco hopes that a Mexican clientele will justify spending surplus money on this service, which is viewed as a luxury item. Because of migration, Tepatitlán, the largest city in the region of Los Altos — the city adjacent to Arandas where Taylor conducted his research — is known as the "migrant city." The upper-class neighborhood Beverly Tepa is named after Beverly Hills. The desire to own a wristwatch has been replaced by more extravagant ambitions with higher stakes, such as owning a home in Beverly Tepa. Building in Mexico is not just about material gain; through construction, migrants are engaging decades of ambivalence by dwelling psychologically in both places at once. [Figure 4]

Importantly, money and materials are not only flowing into Mexico. In the 1970s, a Texan family with ties to Mexico built a home in Corpus Christi with stone quarried in Zacatecas. Both the cantera stone and skilled labor had to be imported. The family relied on the help of a family in Mexico and endured a lengthy process to acquire work visas and permits to bring the stone north. Since the 1980s small family businesses primarily owned by Mexicans emerged throughout the Southwest to facilitate the importation of cantera. Individuals now work with hundreds of artisanal stonemasons throughout Mexico and scores of quarries in approximately a dozen Mexican states to facilitate the realization of "Mexican-style" or "hacienda-style" homes in the US, primarily commissioned by Mexican and Mexican-American clientele. Largely outside of large-scale businesses and corporations, individuals build networks that span territories to create and shape built environments on both sides of the boundary. [Figure 5]

The Mexican North and the US South — indeed, many places throughout the two nations and the Americas — are littered with evidence of migrants' lasting attachment to hometowns as they sow new roots in host cities. The spaces of migration — whether they be the interiors of migrant dream homes or aspirational businesses — reveal that migrants are not necessarily choosing between two or more places; rather, they are intensifying their relationships, connections and networks to multiple localities. Analysis of places like Texas and Jalisco as being inextricably linked allows us to perceive not only what the costs of these trends are for those making the most sacrifices but also the complexity of these places themselves, which are increasingly defined by mobile populations, building for a life of movement rather than a life of stasis.

Notes

1. The Social Science Research Council was then a privately funded organization whose mission was to study the scientific aspects of human migration.
2. In the 1920s Taylor recorded the wage rates of several participants in his study on Mexican labor in the United States. His findings illustrate a wide range of potential earnings. For example, in 1929 one man received 35 and 40 cents per hour working on the railroad, whereas coal-mining, steel, or car manufacturing wages were in some cases as high as 6, 7, or even 9 US dollars per day (12, 14, and 18 pesos,

respectively). See Paul S. Taylor, *A Spanish-Mexican Peasant Community: Arandas in Jalisco, Mexico* (Berkeley: University of California Press, 1933), 25. Yet Taylor also claims that even as early as the 1930s people were going to the United States "not from economic necessity, but to *aventurar* in the United States." Ibid., 40.

3. Manuel Gamio's work has been extensively published. See Manuel Gamio, *Mexican Immigration to the United States: A Study of Human Migration and Adjustment* (Chicago: University of Chicago Press, 1930), and "Notes Gathered for His Book, Mexican Migration to the United States, and Related Material, 1926–1928," Bancroft Library, University of California, Berkeley.
4. Taylor continued studying Mexican migration as one of his lifelong interests. The Bancroft Library has an extensive collection of field notes, correspondence, interviews and more. On Mexican migration and place, see Taylor's *Spanish-Mexican Peasant Community*. For a more general discussion of migration, see his *Mexican Labor in the United States,* 3 vols. (Berkeley: University of California Press, 1928–34).
5. "Immigrants Send Less Money Home," *New York Times*, July 3, 1930.
6. While these are the first studies to analyze what migrants brought with them across the US–Mexico boundary, thus leaving the question open as to when these practices began, the Gamio and Taylor manuscripts document emergent changes, suggesting the relative newness of the practice of remitting objects alongside dollars in the 1920s and 1930s.
7. Taylor, *Spanish-Mexican Peasant Community*.
8. Ibid., 57.
9. Ibid, 56. According to Taylor, customary local dress included the palm sombrero, the cotton *camisa* and *calzones* (cotton shirt and trousers) and *guaraches*. For Sundays the returned emigrants, both in town and from the ranches, sometimes wore tailored or ready-made suits and the hats and shoes that they had brought back from the United States.
10. Aside from road building, Taylor notes that overall factories were built in response to the demand for overalls. This spatial change was most likely an isolated occurrence. It does, however, suggest that the built environment of Mexico was responding to migration in several ways.
11. Gamio, *Mexican Immigration,* 225.
12. Ibid, 68.
13. An album of Gamio's photographs, *Fotografias diversas correspondientes a la colonia Acambaro,* is available at the Bancroft Library, UC Berkeley.
14. Taylor, *Spanish-Mexican Peasant Community,* 63.
15. Ibid., 58. This comment can be contrasted to another of Taylor's anecdotes: "I talked with repatriates — one of them from Mason City, Iowa. He had returned with savings of $3,000 and was living in ease on his father's ranch with part of his savings out at interest of one and one-half percent per month." See Paul Taylor, "Vignettes from Old Mexico," *University of California Chronicle* (April 1932): 128.
16. Taylor, *Spanish-Mexican Peasant Community*, 54. In Gamio's study, an interviewee expresses the opposite sentiment: "I would rather cut my throat before changing my Mexican nationality. I prefer to lose with Mexico than to win with the United States. My country is before everything else and although it has been many years since I have gone back I am only waiting until conditions get better, until there is absolute peace before I go back. I haven't lost hope of spending my last days in my own country." See Gamio, "Notes Gathered."
17. Taylor, *Spanish-Mexican Peasant Community*, 52.
18. Taylor, "Vignettes from Old Mexico."
19. Paul S. Taylor, "Perspectives on Mexican-Americans," unpublished essay, 6, in Paul S. Taylor papers, Bancroft Library, University of California, Berkeley.
20. Sarah L. Lopez, "The Remittance House: Architecture of Migration," *Buildings & Landscapes: Journal of the Vernacular Architecture Forum* 17, no. 2 (Fall 2010): 33–52.
21. In the emigrant region of Los Altos, "*estilo Californiano*" or "California-style" is a colloquial phrase used to signify architectural design influenced by what locals perceive to be Californian architecture.
22. For an in-depth study of this topic see Sarah L. Lopez, *The Remittance Landscape: Spaces of Migration in Rural Mexico and Urban USA* (Chicago: University of Chicago Press, 2015).

THE KEY TO SUCCESS IS BEING IN
THE RIGHT PLACE AT THE RIGHT TIME

ALEJANDRO LUPERCA

EL PASO, TEXAS / CIUDAD JUÁREZ, CHIHUAHUA

106.48°

As I wrote this text, social networks were circulating the harrowing image of Óscar and Valeria, a father and daughter from El Salvador, drowned as they tried to cross the Río Bravo. The interim director of the Office of Customs and Border Protection (CBP) resigned after the conditions in which at least 300 minors are being held in a detention center in El Paso, Texas, were made public. On the Mexican side of the border, the National Guard has taken up position and the flow of migrants has fallen. The city has become militarized once again.

What an uncomfortable phrase: "being in the right place at the right time." The right place is the Ciudad Juárez–El Paso border, and the right time was the years 2008 to 2017, from when I embarked on a degree in theory of art until when I decided to move elsewhere. To put this into context, in just the first four years of this period, more than 9,000 homicides were recorded in the city, considered one of the most violent in the world. In 2015 the US State Department even issued travel advisories on the risks of traveling to Mexico, with Juárez receiving special attention. Today, you can see barricades and barbed wire at the international bridges that the *migra* has put in place to ensure that the entry points are not rushed by large numbers of people trying to cross into the United States illegally. For the first time, Hugs Not Walls, an annual binational event that allowed separated families on both sides of the border to meet for a few minutes, was canceled, as it was no longer considered safe by US authorities.

In the face of this desperate panorama, what possibility of success can be found in these places and times? A Little Cuba has sprung up in the historical downtown, where migrants awaiting answers to their asylum applications prepare delicious meals; the hotels are busy again and Facebook's marketplace thrives with new services: "Save yourself the five-hour queue, we'll take you across on motorcycle. We'll leave you where you can take the bus, includes water or orange juice" — a service that costs twenty dollars. The economy is thriving.

Although the wall is ever more imposing and aggressive, the dynamics, effects and affects of the border become more confused and blurred. I remember the same level of media coverage when

Pope Francis visited the city and held mass on a podium looking over the Río Bravo, and when Juan Gabriel died a day before giving a concert in El Paso, Texas. To paraphrase Roberto Bolaño's *2666*, the border is an "oasis of horror in the middle of a desert of boredom"— but above all the border is a space of resilience.

Border Art: Four Cases

I would like to talk about what it means to produce contemporary art on the border with reference to four artists that I had the opportunity to work with. Juárez–Hell Paso has long had a close relationship with art, though often a conflictive one. Its condition as a hyper-mediatized border has made it vulnerable to poverty and to spectacle. It should be no surprise that there is widespread suspicion on the part of the community toward any intervention, artistic or otherwise, that might become a product for global exportation.

How to produce art in the face of the danger of aestheticization? In the face of what José Luis Brea calls "the absolute death certificate of any possibility of thinking about moral, ethical value, in substantive terms, the definitive consecration of a way of thinking about culture and its achievements only as a pure alibi and endorsement of a program that hides — in the marked letter of his defense of the 'insurmountable pluralism of interests and interpretations' and in his affirmation of the fragmentation of the forms of experiences — his best strategy to protect and secure the privileges of domination of those who hold them, to protect and ultimately secure the mere survival of the *status quo*, the positive structural continuity of the established?"[1] I have found the answer in other types of economies: libidinal economies in which "the unpaid work of the affections tirelessly ruins the insulting pyramid of capitalist values"[2]; and above all, in the enunciation of the everyday, of those spaces that remain between the lines, in the memory, in the anecdotal.

Irrigation

In 2010 a schoolmate and I crossed the Córdova-Americas International Bridge — the "Puente Libre"— carrying a number of sheets. "What do you have there? Where are you going?" asked the officer. "We have dirty laundry; we're going to wash it." We were headed to Marfa, three hours from El Paso, together with artist Teresa Margolles. The sheets were impregnated with earth, blood and other bodily secretions recovered from crime scenes in Juárez, where 500 people had been murdered in the first three months of that year. Her performance piece *Irrigation* consisted of a water truck spraying the highways of Texas between Alpine and Marfa with water in which the sheets had been soaked. In a gold Suburban, we filmed this journey of 5,000 gallons. For Teresa, this was a form of returning Texas's waste products back to Texas — the state that exports the most firearms into Mexico.

The Mexican artist usually works in two ways: transfiguration and physical displacement of raw materials that takes on a new meaning. Her works include concrete benches mixed with organic remains or windows steeped in the sweat and grease of young Mexicans. She deals with making visible a concealed reality by exporting it to the circuits of contemporary art.

Apart from the hard work involved in producing this mixture of earth and blood, I'll never forget the return journey. I was an art student, and it was the first time I was working as an artist's assistant, the first time I could walk at night in an unknown town without the fears I was used to. We were listening to Johnny Cash and then, at the moment of crossing back into Juárez, I again felt the fear of the militarized state in which we lived.

A few months later, I was driving in the city with a friend when we were stopped at a military checkpoint. "We're artists," I said. The attitude of the soldiers changed and they became hostile. This is a city, after all, where there is a criminal gang that goes by the name Artistas Asesinos (Killer Artist).

Ciudad Juárez Projects

"Stop playing around, kids!" we heard from the loudspeaker of a municipal police car in downtown Juárez, a few meters from the Paso del Norte International Bridge, while artist Francis Alÿs kicked at a soccer ball in flames and my father ran to put it out with an aluminum bucket. The flaming ball lit up the abandoned bars and hotels that were later demolished by the government to clean up the image of the city. In their place today is the Plaza Juan Gabriel.

Ciudad Juárez Projects is a series of works by Alÿs. The works were undertaken over the course of multiple visits between 2013 and 2014, in the historical district of Juárez, close to Calle Mariscal along the international border, and in residential areas in the southern fringes of the city. The project also accompanies a video from the series *Children's Games*, in which a group of children play at shooting each other with sunrays reflected off mirrors held in their hands, while they play hide-and-seek among abandoned houses.

I'll never forget how the children played happily as their mothers chatted about the medications that their children needed due to trauma suffered "after what happened to their fathers" and the absence of these fathers, though no further details were given.

For a few moments we didn't think about the context we were in — one of survival. Francis and I were using a video camera, innocently recording the stray dogs, the facades and a park where children played on swings in the distance. Suddenly a patrol car turned up, the cops pointing their weapons at us. What was a "gringo" of near two meters in height doing filming these kids? The city's not ready for this, I remembered. This was something I had forgotten before, when near the Santa Teresa International Crossing I drove my car in circles at midnight in order to light up the border wall and get a good shot. What would have happened if the *migra* took photographs of my license plates, as they surely could? How to carry on day by day with projects that so completely break with our everyday notions of caution?

Volveré y Seré Millones (I Will Return and I Will Be Millions)

We follow the borderline along the highway on the US side. I see hundreds of tumbleweeds that have become trapped in the red steel of the wall. A typical plant of the desert that also became emblematic in the cinema of the Wild West. In Juárez they are known as *brujas*, "witches." What an appropriate name and image for this direct relationship with hunting, judgment and condemnation of the migrants between countries, and the distortion of the desert as a space both solitary and caricatured.

In December 2017 we drove this highway for three days. In Juárez–El Paso, Acuña–Del Río and Piedras Negras–Eagle Pass, the phrase *"Volveré y Seré Millones"* ("I Will Return and I Will Be Millions") could be seen at the border crossings. The project involved the temporary installation of a huge, white banner with the phrase printed in black letters. The banner was installed on the Mexican side of the border, but was clearly visible to the border patrol officers posted on the other side of the international bridge. It was also visible for those crossing on foot where the mass deportations take place.

The phrase was uttered by Eva Perón in the early 1950s and later popularized by young left-wing Peronists in artist Enrique Ježik's native Argentina. But the origin of the phrase dates much further back in South American history, and is first attributed to Túpac Amaru II, the Peruvian indigenous leader who led a rebellion against the Spaniards in 1781 and who was subsequently brutally executed, hung and drawn and quartered in a public plaza with parts of his body dispersed across the country. It is said that before the executioner cut out his tongue, Amaru pronounced the phrase in both Spanish and Quechua: "Tikrashami hunu makanakuypi kasha."

Ježik takes up this emblematic slogan from the history of Latin America, placing it in the contemporary landscape of the US–Mexico border. In doing so, he connects the forced repatriation of undocumented migrants to centuries of popular struggle and resistance across the continent.

Border Tuner

We are in a building looking over the Plaza de Los Lagartos in downtown El Paso. We are waiting for two officers from US Border Patrol in order to explain to them Rafael Lozano-Hemmer's project to create an installation on both sides of the border. As they use the virtual reality simulator, I see how the agents are fascinated by the technology; the cabins used by the military to control drones also come to my mind.

Border Tuner is a large-scale participatory art installation by the Mexico-born Lozano-Hemmer. It is designed to interconnect El Paso and Ciudad Juárez and to emphasize the complex and lasting collaboration that exists between the two cities and the two countries, providing a powerful and positive counternarrative to the current rhetoric on the border. The piece will be installed in both countries and includes powerful robotic reflectors that create bridges of light that open live sound channels in order to communicate across the border.

The lights can be adjusted by visitors at six interactive stations, three located in Parque Chamizal in Juárez and three in Bowie High School in El Paso. Each of the interactive stations has a custom lectern with a microphone, a speaker and a control knob. When two lights meet in the sky and cross, a sound channel opens up between people in the two remote stations. As they speak and listen, the brightness of the bridge of light modulates in synchrony, a flash like a flicker of Morse code.

The first day that Rafael came to the border, his plan was to create another wall, but discovering the city and speaking to people changed his perspective. The premise of the project is to form connections between the communities on both sides of the border and to make visible existing relationships: expanding connections and the shared culture. The work seeks to provide a platform for a wide range of local voices and an opportunity to attract international attention to the cooperation and interdependence of the sister cities that together form the largest binational metropolitan area in the Western Hemisphere.

Producing in Post-~~Poverty~~ Misery

I chose to discuss these four projects because they changed my way of thinking about the city, about my role as a producer and as a person, because they had a positive effect on the region and those involved, and because they are by artists who have genuinely involved themselves on different scales with the Other. They are exemplary projects that can help us rethink how we can contribute to the development of a city. We were in the right place at the right time.

Many international artists who seek to produce authentic, relevant art that is rooted in this urban landscape require the contribution and guidance of the people who call this border city their home. We become a tool, as cultural intermediaries and translators, responding to the objectives and means of the artists, with its people, places, landscapes and activities that provide the context for an authentic, well-founded response to the reality of the border.

Countless young Juárez artists have taken on this role as mediator. Often the artistic processes that take place are a reflection of the production processes of the assembly plant industry — that is, foreign agents employing local labor in the manufacture or production of art works, which are exported to museums in Mexico City, the United States or Europe. Often, the artists' assistants and other local people involved in these works don't even have the chance to experience the product in its final form, as it is assembled, finished and exhibited elsewhere. In this type of process, the objects and ideas created in response to the city have no practical function here, are not connected to the border itself, and do not change, improve or affect the lives of the people living here.

— June 2019

Notes

1. José Luis Brea, "La estetización difusa de las sociedades actuales y la muerte tecnológica del arte." Available at: http://www.fadu.edu.uy/estetica-diseno-ii/files/2018/03/brea-estetizaci%C3%B3n-difusa.pdf, accessed July 27, 2020. Translation the author's.
2. Claire Fontaine, *Notas sobre economía libidinal* (Castilla y León: MUSAC, 2011), 42–43.

HACKABLE INFRASTRUCTURES

ERSELA KRIPA

EL PASO, TEXAS / CIUDAD JUÁREZ, CHIHUAHUA

106.48°

The US–Mexico border is defined by a surveillance apparatus of physical and virtual infrastructures that control all forms of life within the border region. The movement of bodies is documented, catalogued and transmitted to policing institutions whose operating policy is to capture and punish. Sophisticated mechanisms scan the territory to routinely filter information into various categories of threat, parsed as "documented" or "undocumented." In this highly controlled environment, the geography, geology and meteorology are instrumentalized for purposes of controlling cross-border flows. These instruments suggest an all-encompassing definition of infrastructure as an evolved system of control, where historical divisions between physical infrastructure, geological formations, aeolian flows and human activity no longer exist.

In more central locations, while infrastructure is shaped by unprecedented population growth, it is similarly governed by equally paranoid desires of control. In high-density urban centers, where robust systems handle high volumes of movement, physical forms of infrastructure are augmented by intelligent virtual systems. These systems are designed to evolve in immaterial form, functioning independently of human input. Keller Easterling posits infrastructure as a form of power through which nonstate actors direct policy and forge international political alliances in the drive for profit. Consequently, the operational materiality of infrastructure evades definition and becomes imperceptible. In this context, the question is "how do we resist these invisible control mechanisms without having access to this information?"

Whereas, historically, infrastructure was constructed as a public works endeavor to facilitate material and bodily flows, its recent version is mostly dedicated to the collection and processing of the information that measures those flows. The material inertia of bridges, dams, aqueducts and walls has been augmented, and in some instances wholly replaced, by the invisible digital fluency of virtual footprints, RFID passports, global passes, credit scores and data transmittance.[1] This immaterial, "soft" infrastructure is both evasive and pervasive — more agile and potentially more impactful than its historically physical counterpart. As millions of bodies move through digital gates, this "software" spatially constrains

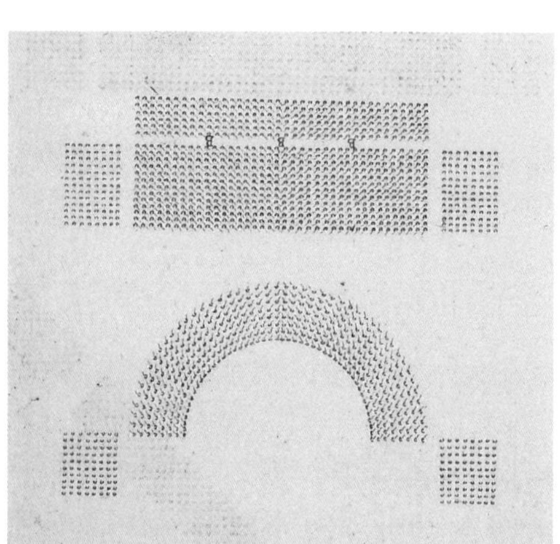

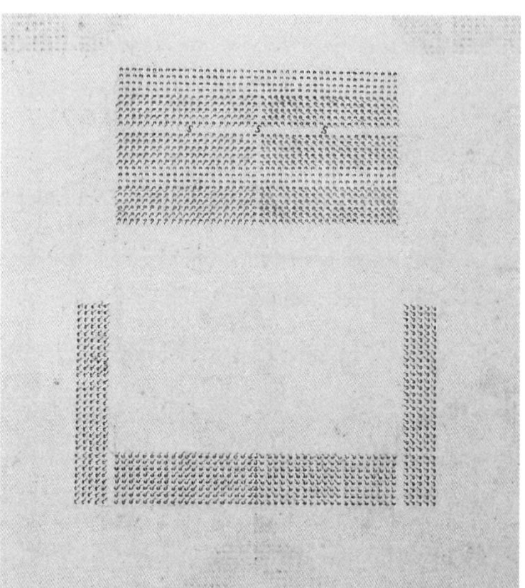

Andrea Palladio, Studies of Infantry Formations Confronting Each Other. Image courtesy: The Provost and Fellows of Worcester College, Oxford.

Andrea Palladio, *Battle of Palermo*. Polybius, *Histories*. The relationship between constructed infrastructure and ephemeral formations of bodies allowed for the expansion of defensive strategies beyond the boundaries of the fortress.

and directs their lives, dictating their futures by converting processed beings into data that can be sorted and packaged for sale to the highest bidder.

The history of civilizations is directly related to the rise and fall of their infrastructural systems. In cities, where empires, and later nations, concentrated their governance, the construction of robust infrastructure was necessary to maintain biopolitical control. The Romans, for instance, expanded their empire by building roads to connect colonies to major trade route networks while simultaneously isolating their city within a sophisticated system of walls. Acting as the first line of defense, the walls naturally became targets of military attacks. To this end, military leaders engaged architects to design protective infrastructures and to anticipate their weaknesses. By using projective drawings, architects iterated through geometries that were most suitable for strategic protection while capable of resisting invasion. The geometry of the fortress afforded directionality of surveillance and allowed for the control of material and bodily movements at dedicated openings. The resulting radially folded floor plan was an infrastructural system typology designed to anticipate the attacker exclusively in its own organizational logic — its spatially defined geometries projected similarly spatial responses by invading armies.

Bodies vs. Walls

During the Renaissance, the prominent rise of the architect's role in shaping the city was paralleled by his efforts to protect its physical boundaries. Working iteratively, architects designed impenetrable walls, tested them for potential failures and planned for their breach. This line of thinking within the architectural discipline actively borrowed from military theory in order to contribute to its own spatial evolution. In a perfect feedback loop, the designer of the defense infrastructure was also the producer of breach tactics. One of the most prominent architects and scholars of the Italian Renaissance, Andrea Palladio, spent forty years researching and drawing the military histories of Julius Caesar and Polybius in two detailed volumes. Of specific interest are Palladio's etchings of battle formations illustrating the

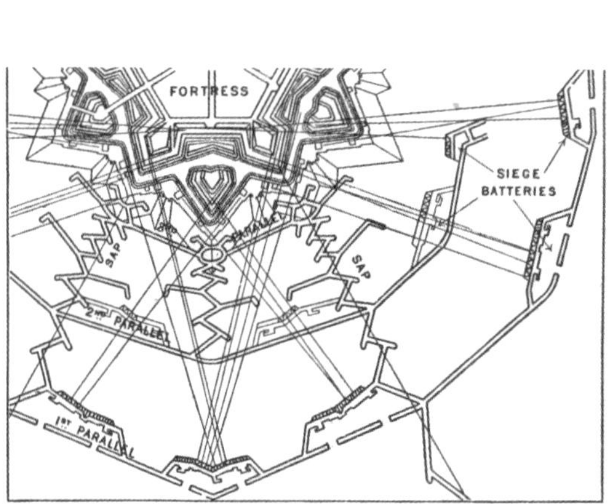

FIG. 12.—REGULAR ATTACK ON A FORTRESS (VAUBAN'S SYSTEM)

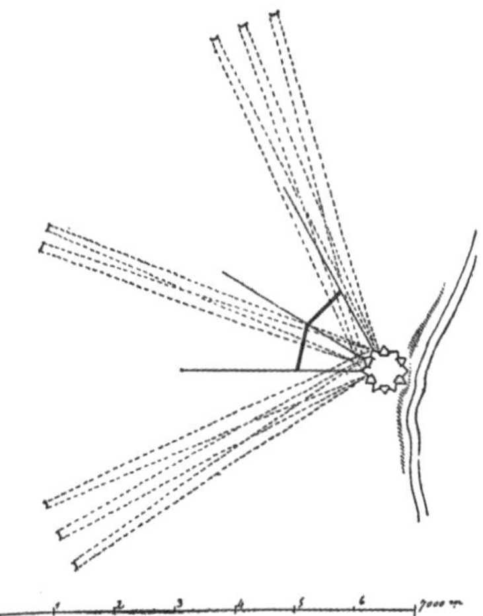

While Vauban inscribes the territory with the choreography of bodies through a temporal shaping of response (left), le-Duc expands it outward by maximizing the fortress's visual control from a static position. Images: open source.

Physical models of Vauban's siegecraft, Musée des Plans-Reliefs. Photograph by author.

narrations of Polybius's *Histories*,[2] where a direct relationship between the formal aspects of infrastructure and the respective battle configurations is immediately visible. His formation drawings organize bodies in geometrically defined assemblages in opposition to the material assemblage of the embattlement walls. By equally detailing the relational logics among bodies and the architecture of fortification, Palladio places them in equal footing, destabilizing the perceived power of infrastructure. The human army becomes a geometrically defined counterinfrastructure.

The evolution of the complexity of battle formations, which responded directly to the changing infrastructural typologies they were designed to overtake, highlights the intimate relationship between organized bodies and infrastructural logic. In its most physical form, infrastructure controls movement and defends the space of the territory, and it requires an equally spatial operation if it is to be overtaken by a phalanx. In Palladio's studies, the specificity of civic structures effected strategic formations that privileged the overall formal configurations of predetermined geometries — the familiar star-shaped closed wall. These rigorous formations were to be maintained regardless of the temporal unfolding of battle, favoring the determinism of infrastructural form rather than temporally fluid events. However, while the fortress continued to be the primary system of protection, designers and engineers updated their disciplinary thinking in response to military innovations. In the seventeenth and eighteenth centuries, French engineer Sébastien Le Prestre de Vauban was instrumental in updating the geometry of the fortress as well as predicting its penetrability. His idea of protectionism relied on walls, and he famously proposed that France give up its indefensible territories in order to maintain a continuous border wall. Unlike Palladio, Vauban's siegecraft drawings mark a transition from a purely strategic attack toward a tactical operation where battalions organize in smaller groupings, which are more agile and relate to each other as time unfolds. This moment signals a shift in military theory where the control of bodies becomes topically relational and formations anticipate a smart and elusive infrastructure.

In the nineteenth century, French architect Eugène Viollet-le-Duc[3] designed a series of fortresses that rethink the art of battle as an evolutionary model; in so doing, he anticipated smart operations. In *Histoire d'une Forteresse*, a fictional history about the attack of an imaginary town, he speculated on the changing geometries of the material configuration of a town's fortress in relationship to the introduction of smart weapons — as well as its connection to specific terrain. He argued that both tactical and strategic games needed to be played in order for the protective wall to hold. As battle tactics evolved in response to increased infrastructural complexity, Viollet-le-Duc also documented the reverse effect: how smart weaponry and formations affected infrastructure and potentially caused it to evolve.

Bodies vs. Portals

A century later, as infrastructure is emancipated from physical material toward a more supple ambiguity, the organization of relationships among bodies is trapped and controlled by its intangible logics. The dematerialization of infrastructure continues, especially in densifying megacities, where people build their environments on their own behalf. As the world's population continues to grow and resources diminish, the fight for access to infrastructural amenities will become fiercer. In order to survive, self-organized informal communities rely on hacking energy flows from formal systems, which are slow to adapt to growing demands. While the physical manifestation of infrastructure in megacities remains obdurate, its software is increasingly able to control bodies via elusive digitized gates that are capable of organizing material as well as data flows at unprecedented speeds. Physical ports, dams and highways provide certain stability and a tangible way of hacking, but the immaterial form of infrastructure increasingly controls territories untethered from a locality. The location of data storage infrastructure is entirely extraneous to the physical expression of its impact; for instance, a computer that checks passports for border-crossing may have its database miles away from the actual border. The spatial split between the material form of infrastructure and its powerful effects fosters a pervasive control apparatus that destabilizes ontological understandings of physical defensive barriers. As information is distributed in computational nodes of networks, the power structures that regulate it are equally deterritorialized, consolidating control extrajurisdictionally.

Bodies vs. Flows

The elusive form of twentieth- and twenty-first-century infrastructure relies on the meteorological space that surrounds it. Air is charged with visible and invisible material, airborne particulates, active chemicals and information signals — all orbiting above their origin centers creating a layered territory defined by entangled jurisdictional ambiguity. As winds displace airborne materials, it becomes impossible to identify who owns which air. How can sites where air originates be held accountable for their microbodies that travel to distant regions? Conversely, how can those affected by airborne flows control the impacts on their bodies, health and rights? The ability to access information of airborne matter can decide the difference between power and powerlessness, and even between life and death.

In this context, information warfare coupled with airborne contamination offers a new version of power dynamics. Since WWII militaries have blurred national and jurisdictional boundaries to gain advantage by using prevailing winds to distribute deadly gases.[4] Practices of spraying pesticides, like Agent Orange during the Vietnam War, or cloud seeding, continue to be perfected and more sophisticated. Currently, as part of airstrike training, the US military has incorporated soft sensing sites at training installations that prepare army and first responder trainees to contain biological and chemical matter in a WMD scenario. At the Dugway Proving Ground training installation in Utah, for instance, trainees are taught how to collect, test and protect against airborne warfare.[5] People's powerlessness against an airborne chemical attack suggests that perhaps the most insidious type of warfare is the uncoupling of physical infrastructure from its effects. While world militaries continue their twofold arms race — to defend their data infrastructure and to destroy that of others — the civilian lives it affects are caught in the cross fire. In order to gain access to the invisible information flows a kind of hacking is necessary for those who are counted as collateral damage. Hacking becomes an important act of resistance.

Nephelometry: a dust sensor network along the US–Mexico border. Low-cost dust sensor bundles are housed within 3-D-printed housing hacking surveillance cameras in order to collect information on air pollution. The mappings produced by the measurements defy the singular line of the border wall, highlighting the shared airshed and ecological damage in the border region due to infrastructural and environmental neglect.
Project: Ersela Kripa & Stephen Mueller, AGENCY.

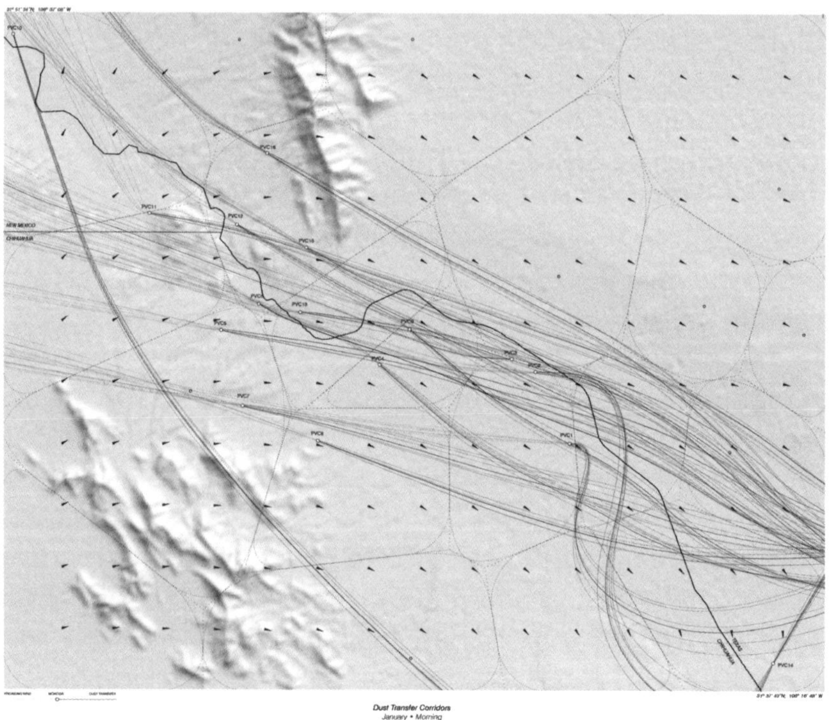

Bodies vs. Barriers

The urgency of the need to access information is acutely catalyzed on the US–Mexico border, where surveillance and data collection enacts national military policy, controlling bodies with targeted precision. Data signals, radio frequencies and scanning waves are mixed with particulate matter and pollutants, thickening the air of the borderlands. The region is part of the Chihuahuan Desert, where high-velocity winds trigger dangerous levels of dust pollution, particularly during the spring season. Additionally, the deteriorating air quality in El Paso and Ciudad Juárez is related to the rampant development of free economic zones supported by the border condition and low-wage factory production. Multinational corporations exploit cheap labor while causing deep environmental damage without accountability. While government-sponsored air-quality monitoring stations collect data, they do not disseminate it to the local population. The collection stations tend to average regional air-quality data, which does not precisely highlight local dust issues. Consequently, the bodies of factory workers who are exploited for low-cost production are also neglected and physically damaged by the withholding of information. As their lungs malfunction and their children fall ill, communities are unable to fight for change without tangible proof of the data of the particulates they breathe. The highly sophisticated infrastructural system of the border controls life at all levels, from basic access at checkpoints to the right to a healthy body, exercising biopolitical power in its purest form. In this one-directional information structure, the architect can intervene to once again find its weaknesses, to reestablish the human body with equal agency against the infrastructures of control.

Nephelometry

The project, titled *Nephelometry — Drawn Across Borders,* uses a network of low-cost dust sensors to measure the presence of particulate matter and to track its movement across the binational boundary. The sensors are installed on both sides of the border in homes whose inhabitants responded to a word-of-mouth announcement. Consequently, the unplanned distribution of data collection points is localized to communities with the highest air-quality concerns. As winds shift hourly, responsibilities and consequences of pollution are buried in the messy coexistence of local, city, state, federal and international regulations, all of which do not neatly coincide. Drawings of the movement of particulates throughout the day reveal a continuously shifting mass of information in the air that belongs to both nations, ignoring the border wall. Working at the territorial scale while zooming in to the building scale, the drawings interrogate the stubbornness of the infrastructure of "defense" in the context of shifting geographical characteristics.

The sensors transmit data to an online platform that allows individuals to see precisely the amount of dust they breathe at a given time. Each sensor is geolocated and is easily transportable to anyone interested in measuring their air. The project is an accessible parallel to the highly controlled and opaque binational monitoring infrastructure between the United States and Mexico. The sensors are located in underserved neighborhoods, in mostly self-organized and self-built informal communities. In this context, individuals hack their infrastructures daily, rewriting their codes and procedures to achieve equity, to force transparency and to enable new forms of dialogue and production. This project functions at the locus where hacker culture meets the city, cataloguing, analyzing and co-opting ways in which we, the citizens, intersect with urban systems. The collected data is broadcast in real time on an online site effectively democratizing access to information, rendering the physical border barrier a mute relic of the past. As information flows through the fence, the air that hosts it gains new agency in architecture's quest to dismantle physical infrastructures of exclusion and control.

Notes

1. See Keller Easterling, *Enduring Innocence: Global Architecture and its Political Masquerades* (Cambridge: MIT Press, 2007).
2. See Guido Beltramini, *Andrea Palladio and the Architecture of Battle* (Venice: Marsilio, 2010).
3. Eugene Emmanuel Viollet-Le-Duc, *Annals of a Fortress: Twenty-Two Centuries of Siege Warfare* (Mineola: Dover Publications, 2007), 363.
4. See Peter Sloterdijk, *Terror from the Air* (Los Angeles: Semiotext(e), 2009).
5. Bonnie A. Robinson, "Dugway Offers Global Chemical-Biological Response Training," *Dugway News*, February 5, 2018: https://www.dugway.army.mil/NewsArticle.aspx?articleId=/PAO/Articles/2018/02/MobileTrainingTeams.htm.

EL PASO, TEXAS

IWAN BAAN

106.48°

EL PASO, TEXAS

EL PASO, TEXAS

EL PASO, TEXAS

JRZ
ELP

EL PASO, TEXAS

EL PASO, TEXAS

Bienvenidos

EL PASO, TEXAS

106.48°

EL PASO, TEXAS

106.48°

EL PASO, TEXAS

106.48°

EL PASO, TEXAS

EL PASO, TEXAS

ONLY
RIGHT LANE
MUST
TURN RIGHT
Executive
Ctr Blvd

SMELTER
1882 CEMETERY 1970

EL PASO, TEXAS

106.48°

AIRBORNE AGENTS

STEPHEN MUELLER

EL PASO, TEXAS / CIUDAD JUÁREZ, CHIHUAHUA

106.48°

Dust knows no borders. Dust storms throughout borderland desert regions routinely transgress national boundaries and other jurisdictional divides.[1, 2] These massive particulate flows impact the operations and spatial mechanisms of the expanding securocratic[3] territory of the American Southwest, spawning new relationships between airborne particulate and security forces throughout the region. In border agent training sites and specialized military installations, operatives rehearse strategies and adopt technologies to mitigate the impact of airborne dust on security objectives while simultaneously weaponizing its effects. Transnational airborne geologies forge new cross-boundary alliances, expanding the seemingly certain bright line of the international border in a thickened, ever-shifting, particulate-laden atmosphere.

Dust in the borderland indexes: a spreading constellation of desert security training sites constituting a new form of meteorological urbanism; an escalating practice of exploiting extant aeolian landforms to enact atmospheric simulations conducive to desert security training; and the growing prevalence of specialized, materially intensive training landscapes that harvest airborne particulate, exploit it as an asset and deploy it to enact transformational territorial flows.

Meteorological Occupations

A growing tactical concern with airborne particulate has transformed the desert territories of the American Southwest and northern Mexico. A growing number of military and security training sites in the borderland are strategically sited within particular geographies severely impacted by windblown dust, yielding far-reaching constellations of discrete and diverse interventions conditioned by binational atmospheric conditions. These meteorological occupations each opportunistically exploit material resonances within larger transboundary fields of weather, geology and landform and serve as evidence of nascent logics of expansive territorial geoegineering of the borderland in support of security objectives.

Desert landscapes and remote geographies have long been used by the US military, which leverages the elemental exposure the sites provide to enhance training exercises. The California-Arizona Maneuver Area (CAMA) offers an early example, claiming over thirteen million acres across California, Nevada and Arizona to prepare troops and equipment for combat in the similarly harsh arid environments they were likely to encounter in battle zones in WWII.[4] Through the training on-site and beyond, these expansive militarized areas have served as testing grounds for a sophisticated form of security-driven territorial geoengineering. Training exercises exploit the landform to concoct imaginary conflictual confluences of atmosphere, geology and state power, intersecting in the blinding dust and radiant heat of desert landscapes. An early simulated conflict at CAMA, for instance, pitted the fictional nation-states of Calonia and Nezona in a battle over territorial water rights, including the first-ever simulation of civilian control of the military, with officers role-playing prime ministers and cabinet members.[5]

Military strategists began to view the diverse desert atmospheres of the American Southwest as ready-made environmental adversaries, developing geostrategic planning efforts to maximize the potential use of the desert environment for training. As CAMA and similar sites claimed vast, immersive desert areas for practical training, the US Army conducted research on the threat of the desert climate to operations and installations.[6] A report from the Earth Sciences Division identifies major geological features and meteorological threats to a range of installations in the American Southwest.[7] The grain character of each site was studied, measured and identified as a material asset or latent liability, revealing the perceived codependence between military training logistics, geology and atmosphere. Building on these early experiments, extensive desert warfare training sites proliferated throughout the US in the latter half of the twentieth century[8, 9] and continue to grow in scale and sophistication to this day.

While the constellation of desert training sites capitalizes on geospecific assets, they fundamentally inscribe the borderland as a georelational territory, a collection of anonymized deserts serving as stand-ins for the forboding, distant geographies of projected future conflict. Enlisting this territory, the military seeks to perfect a predictive model of emissive potential in desert terrain.[10] The US Army obsessively catalogues dust potential[11] globally and makes detailed geological maps in tandem with military operations in order to accurately predict the amount of dust anticipated in particularly dry theaters of operation. A project called the Catalogue of Analogs by the Desert Research Institute (DRI) articulates georelational equivalencies between desert environments in the Southwest and theaters of conflict abroad. Researchers scour the geologic composition of Department of Defense (DoD) inventory to find parallels between soil characteristics on base and those expected in combat zones.[12, 13] Mineral deposits and landforms in the US are shown alongside their geological doppelgangers in Iraq and Afghanistan, ensuring a degree of environmental realism as trainees traverse the landscape. In practice, these equivalencies are played out in the naming and use of the sites. At Yuma Proving Ground (YPG), for instance, there is a specialized training course called the Middle East Desert.[14] Trainees can rest assured that the dust clouds they kick up in southern Arizona will be indistinguishable from those they see once deployed. As training sites have grown and training activities increase in scope, security training exercises which benefit from the

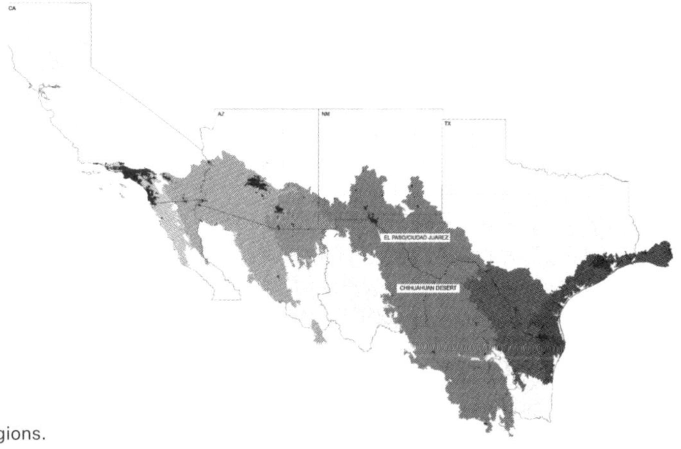

Binational ecoregions.

Dust landing training. Courtesy Defense Visual Information Distribution Service.

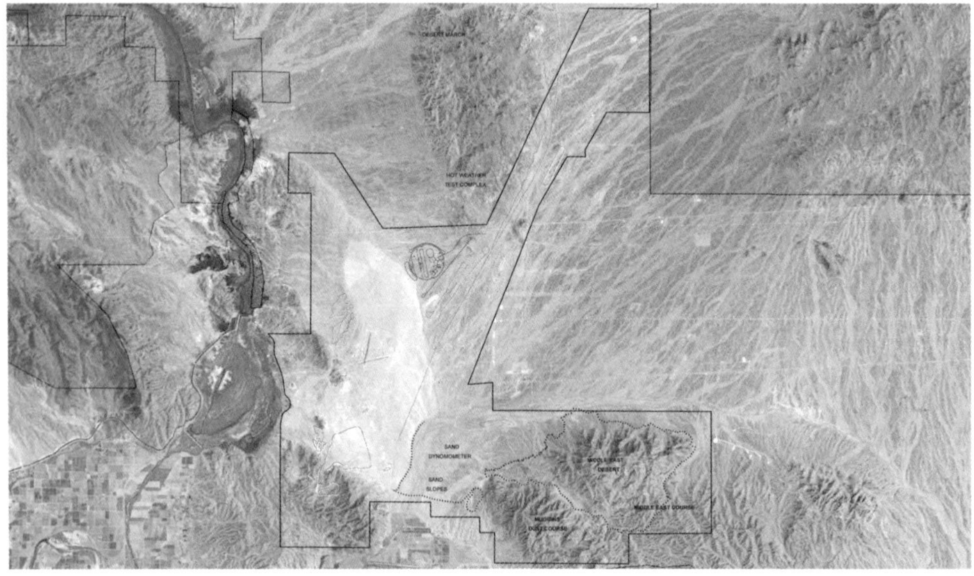

Yuma Proving Grounds desert training environments. Drawing: AGENCY.

borderland desert atmosphere have begun to significantly and detrimentally impact its composition. The US Army has long acknowledged the military's own role in creating dust storms.[15] Training activities contribute substantially to dust transfer[16] in the region along the Southwest border.[17] Dust transfer from desert training sites on base to nearby cities continues to exacerbate tensions between base and city. Airborne dust from training activities and base expansion is a common complaint from nearby civilians.[18] From the base's perspective, the atmospheric by-products of a nearby city may adversely impact its environment, compromising and corrupting its training activities that are so dependent on territorial environmental control.[19, 20]

These pressures have led to even more expansive territorial geoengineering efforts, through which the military has deployed a combination of physical interventions, design guidelines and legal mechanisms, prolonging its occupation of desert environments while mitigating its perceived impact on them. The US Army Corps of Engineers (USACE) studies the dynamics of dune formation to shape and control the elusive landform of the desert.[21] Dr. John Gillies of the Desert Research Institute (DRI) studies methods of mitigating fugitive dust from exercises on military bases in order to improve air quality and maximize training days.[22] He has been able to identify the unique sources of dust emission in the military environment (vehicles, helicopters, weapon blasts) that pose unique challenges, while also studying the impact of base activities on surrounding urban environments.[23] Despite these efforts, "military training grounds in Texas and California consistently produce large regional dust storms that can be seen on satellite imagery."[24] [25, 26] Hydroseeding and dust palliatives are regularly applied to sites expecting heavy equipment in order to lessen the likelihood of airborne dust.[27] Intricate spatial and legal mechanisms for controlling or allowing unwanted aerial intrusions are increasingly proposed. The Whole Building Design Guide (WBDG) issues guidelines for admixtures and other site mitigation techniques on airfields and other DoD installations.[28] It also promotes the use of vegetative windscreens of maximum height and "aerodynamic roughness" on DoD installations to capture fugitive dust.[29] Defense funds are deployed to purchase "avigation easements" from nearby homeowners,[30] allowing the military to define the use and composition of civilian airspace for its own purposes.

The desert training sites of the borderland reflect trends in global urbanization. As urban areas desertify, and desert areas urbanize, the urbanized desert makes its way to the training installations. Over the past two decades, desert training sites have themselves become more urbanized, introducing simulated urban environments to the open desert ranges.[31] The desert is no longer an empty battlefield, but a tissue that connects nodes of urbanization.

In this light, the US–Mexico borderland, as an extant urbanized and urbanizing desert, is becoming a geostrategic readymade for future security and military training operations. In addition to its urban features, substantial layers of security infrastructure grafted within the desert produce atmospheric effects which parallel projected military occupations abroad. The US Marine Corps, for instance, has used border surveillance roads as test sites to study dust palliative measures for applications in Iraq and Afghanistan.[32] The isolated road, arid atmosphere and rhythm of daily patrols conspire to form cycles of dust transfer analogous to those expected in operating bases in theater. While the military benefits from atmospheric effects of the border security apparatus, it also contributes to border security operations. US Marines in Ground Sensor Platoons use stints on the border to prepare for deployment in Afghanistan. As the scrubby desert and mountainous terrain provides a georelational analog for their eventual tour, they assist US Border Patrol in detecting and interdicting migrants crossing the terrain.[33]

To the security apparatus, the borderland appears as an assemblage of open-air environmental laboratories optimized for testing and training its operatives, an actuated atmosphere in which competing flows of airborne particulate, human activity, and technological experimentation are continuously and reliably reproduced.

Atmospheric Simulations

Borderland training sites provide an atmospheric realism essential to training a variety of security operatives. Dust on the sites hinders and telegraphs movement as it simultaneously infiltrates bodies and machines. The "frequent near-blinding dust storms and blazing heat"[34] of the borderland are cited not as detriments, but desirable features, capable of conditioning bodies for deployment in conflict zones, including ongoing operations in the borderland itself. Dust, once thought only a nuisance, here has value in its ability to translocate a distant or projected atmosphere and provide a site for simulation and study. The dust cloud becomes a form of material computation, a physical foil for bodies and machines to spar against. Augmented machines simulate specific and localized bursts of "foreign soil." The presumed negative impact of dust in the region is thus a perverse positive, a "high commodity"[35] suspended in the atmosphere of the sites.[36]

A range of geologically endowed bases, training centers and proving grounds in the region have been established as test beds for developing technologies and systems suitable for the spatial vacuum and blind-out conditions of the desert. Brownout events, in which airborne dust and sand severely limit visibility, are common in conflict zones and deemed critical for military operatives to master. Borderland training sites provide ideal conditions for this type of training, hosting specialized training courses capable of reproducing a sufficiently "degraded visual environment" (DVE) to challenge trainees.

Military vehicles are intentionally subjected to the barrage of windblown dust on a series of "dust courses," developed to withstand an increasingly punishing onslaught of airborne infiltration.[37] Yuma Proving Ground (YPG), in southern Arizona, contains many of these testing grounds.[38] These sites, generally built as "short ovals" on "desert pavement," are meant to parallel the particular geologies of combat theaters.[39] At Yuma, the Kofa and Cibola Dust courses provide slightly different geologic contents, but both are used to evaluate engine filtration systems.[40] The Muggins Mesa Dust Course (MMDC)[41] at YPG was used for decades to test the effects of vehicle-generated dust on equipment. Like other military dust courses, the site represented a finite geological resource, an anomaly in the underlying geology of the base that provided the soil conditions necessary for the testing of air-blown dust.[42] The course was used not only by its stewards in the armed services, but by private automobile manufacturers as well. Auto industry designers would trail prototypes behind larger vehicles, intentionally kicking up a cloud of dust to check for areas of intrusion on their model.[43] With intensive use of the Muggins site, dust resources ran low, forcing the army to source other sites with more "sustainable" supplies of dust.[44] YPG is now testing the next-generation desert vehicle, the Joint Light Tactical Vehicle (JLTV), by subjecting it to a six-hour barrage of silicates before taking it out on range.[45] When the environment itself is unreliable, the sites bring the "dust blasting" inside, creating "on-demand" dust storms in indoor testing facilities.[46]

The training activities on the dust courses and regular convoy movements throughout bases in the binational deserts compound the amount of dust in the borderland atmosphere. To predict and mitigate these activities, the military has developed sophisticated predictive simulations to track incoming and outgoing dust plumes from training activities. Using DUSTRAN[47] and other applications, civilian agencies and individual users can create simulations that deploy both military and civilian vehicles in the georeferenced territory of the borderland. Users can choose to witness the effects of Abrams tanks, HMMWVs (Humvees) and other military vehicle types, as well as a number of civilian vehicles including Chevy and Ford sedans. The simulations thus rehearse the intractable link between military and civilian impacts on borderland atmospheres. Though the program is preloaded with only information within the continental US, users can input soil and vegetation data to get an accurate read on atmospheric transmissions in their area of interest, making cross-border simulations possible.

Suspended dust is a prime component of desert aviation training. The military simulation industry is attempting to bring realistic dust effects to the masses by more accurately simulating dust recirculation effects in widely distributed digital mission simulators.[48] But so far, the realism of the actual material and environmental conditions in a physical training site is considered irreplaceable. Both military and border security agents use borderland training sites to prepare for close-ground maneuvers, takeoffs and landings which could be hampered by dust. Blind-outs threaten helicopter navigation. Specialized dust-landing training uses the dust on military training sites to increase the risk of helicopter landings for so-called environmental training.[49] Landing zones are tilled to increase the likelihood and volume of airborne dust.

US Customs and Border Protection (CBP) uses helicopters to track migrants especially in the inhospitable desert environments of the Southwest border. Helicopter operations here are deemed preferable to ground travel from an environmental standpoint, as they lessen the amount of fugitive dust produced.[50] Howard Aitken, director of air operations for Border Patrol's Yuma sector stresses that the "helicopter's real important to cover the alien tracks without disturbing the environment."[51] Operations typically involve pilots following border surveillance roads at low altitudes, sometimes under fifty feet, in order to conduct patrols and avoid encroaching on military airspace overhead. The travel of patrol helicopters so close to ground contributes directly to dust transfer in the region, often leaving dust clouds in the helicopter's wake. To lessen the impact of surveillance activity, pilots are trained to mitigate fugitive dust by planning their angle of attack for landings.[52]

To track the effects of dust and the effectiveness of operatives in the simulated conditions of training, the sites develop and deploy bespoke atmospheric instrumentation and sensing equipment particular to the particulate. The National Training

Center (NTC) at Fort Irwin was the first to feature a fully instrumented range in their desert warfare training site. Its remoteness, shifting terrain and shifting visibilities provided challenges to human and machine sensors. Modern sites routinely suffer from sensor and camera malfunctions brought on by the dusty environment.[53] With insufficient data available from satellites, many bases have local sensing in place. Four stations on post at Fort Bliss monitor for changing weather conditions to give a broad perspective, but many atmospheric effects are elided. For finer-grained results, the method of detection must change: "point collection" from stationary observation stations will not suffice. The distributed nature and variety of dust sources require mobilized techniques to create a time-based, "on-the-ground" perspective. Researchers have found greater success in a vehicle-mounted sensor technology that collects data on and near unpaved roads.[54]

Particle Paranoia

The sites that emerge within the atomized atmosphere of the borderland reflect an emerging paranoia surrounding microscopic, airborne threats. The same security apparatus that exploits the dust is working to mitigate its impact on the various bodies that comprise it. The blind-out conditions so favored by training regimens require careful and persistent monitoring, as sudden shifts in the desert atmosphere could cause both financial and bodily harm, halting training or contributing to training casualties. Studies conducted at Fort Irwin NTC show that trainees, embedded in the desert for days or weeks at a time, often have health issues like valley fever or fungal infections from the air-blown material.[55]

It is becoming increasingly evident that the particle-laden atmosphere of the borderland has direct impacts on both CBP operations and agent health. CBP pilots trained for borderland interdictions are warned that the work may present several health hazards requiring a level of physical and medical fitness, including working "in dusty conditions."[56] Agents are reporting that constant exposure to dust is making them sick, contributing to infections and other health issues. The outlook of prolonged exposure has forced CBP to take on a more expansive environmental cleanup role in the borderland, that typically city services or national environmental agencies would provide.[57] As the future of prolonged operations in the dusty borderland atmosphere becomes a clearer reality, militarized industries refine their weaponry to ensure border operations are unhindered. Glock is developing a new custom-made handgun specifically for CBP agents, increasing their effectiveness in the dust of the borderland. New, improved dust covers and other environmentally responsive details in the next-generation standard-issue weapon will ensure agents are unhampered in their distribution of lethal force while dust is in the air.[58]

For decades, a long held fantasy has persisted concerning the weaponization of unseen airborne particles as a means to control the Southwest border. In the early 1990s physicist Bill Wattenburg proposed to inundate the border with a dusting of fluorescent particles, enabling border security to track the movement of migrants as they left visible trails of the chemicals behind.[59] Agents would discern the streaking paths of the disturbed inert surveillant aerosol with assistance from lasers and ultraviolet lights while unsuspecting travelers would remain unaware of the chemical tag.

Since these early inceptions of invisible airborne security agents, military and security specialists have continuously advanced the idea of a near-future reality in which distributed sensor networks consisting of billions of microscopic sensors will revolutionize both the potential threats and opportunities in securitized atmospheres. By surreptitiously appropriating, enlisting, and equipping particles suspended in air to sense and transmit data, security operatives will infiltrate and image territories at a scale and resolution previously unimaginable. The Defense Advanced Research Projects Agency (DARPA) has been developing the still nascent "smart dust" technological paradigm for at least the last twenty years.[60] US military analysts project scenarios in which enemy operatives harness this technology against US forces, both in the near and mid-term future.[61] Security researchers believe one of many applications of smart dust tech would be "guarding the vast borders in the American Southwest."[62] The current state and future of this perpetually emerging technology remains unclear.

Presently, the dangers of the borderland atmosphere continue to take their toll on the bodies which inhabit and cross through it. Migrant "caravans" traversing the region are routinely treated for dust-related respiratory illnesses[63] while detained migrants increasingly suffer from dust exposure in makeshift accommodations.[64] As new dust-borne and dust-sensitive technologies develop, they are likely to be tested and deployed on the bodies of the borderland.[65]

Notes

1. Previous research has outlined the many ways in which dust enacts an infrastructural response to global security. See Studio Dust Institute in the Student Index of this volume.
2. A forensic, geospatial investigation of dust transmission in the cross-border region can expose asymmetrical political, economic and regulatory frameworks, revealing the fragile reciprocity of different environments impacted by this airborne, transnational geology. See Ersela Kripa and Stephen Mueller, "Infrastructure of Dust-Managing Particulate in the Borderland," in *Cross Americas: Probing Disglobal Networks*, Proceedings of ACSA Santiago Conference, June 29–July 1, 2016, https://www.acsa-arch.org/chapter/infrastructure-of-dust-managing-particulate-in-the-borderland/, accessed July 27, 2020.
3. A "securocratic" territory is a common geography shaped by shared security interests. Its geographical limits, as well as the limits of what subjects it targets, are by its nature poorly defined.
4. The site set the stage for Desert Strike in 1964 and allowing ongoing preparations for nuclear war. Donald E. Sabol and Eric V. McDonald, *From Army Outpost to Military Training Installations for Worldwide Operations: How WWII Transformed the Military Presence in the Southwestern United States*. Military Geosciences and Desert Warfare (New York: Springer, 2016), 19–35.
5. Harold K. Roach, "The Red Devils in Desert Strike," *Infantry* (January–February 1964): 7–15.
6. US Army Natick Laboratories, Earth Sciences Division, *A Study of Windborne Sand and Dust in Desert Areas* (August 1963), www.dtic.mil/dtic/tr/fulltext/u2/417036.pdf.
7. Ibid.
8. See Ersela Kripa and Stephen Mueller, *FRONTS: Security and the Developing World* (San Francisco: Applied Research and Design, 2020).
9. Desert training began in earnest during WWII.
10. Eric V. McDonald, "Integrated Desert Terrain Forecasting for Military Operations (DTF)," www.dri.edu/earth-ecosystem-sciences/earth-eco-research/1782-integrated-desert-terrain-forecasting-for-military-operations-DoD-desert-terrain, accessed April 7, 2019.
11. Dust potential is often also referred to as *particulate emission potential*, and is qualified largely by soil content and size.
12. McDonald, "Integrated Desert Terrain Forecasting for Military Operations."
13. Recognizing technology transfer between civilian and military dust sensing can be a tool to understanding shared impacts. This period is witness to open-sourcing of previously proprietary atmospheric simulation software, for example, DUSTRAN.
14. US Army, Yuma Proving Ground Integrated Natural Resources Management Plan, 2012, www.yuma.army.mil/docs/YPG_IntegratedNaturalResourcesMgtPln2012.pdf, accessed April 7, 2019.
15. Ibid. Heavy tank movement in Fort Hood and Yuma were said to cause significant dust transport.
16. Dust transfer here refers to aeolian (wind-borne) sediment transport.
17. For example, "Activities at US Department of Defense (DoD) training and testing ranges can be sources of dust into local and regional airsheds governed by air quality regulations. Activities that could disturb the soil surface, and thus generate dust, include vehicle and troop maneuvers, convoy movement, helicopter activities,

munitions impacts, roadway preparations and wind erosion. Other sources of particulates include smokes and obscurants, controlled burns and engine operations." Pacific Northwest National Laboratory, "DUSTRAN System Overview," dustran.pnnl.gov, accessed April 7, 2019.

18. Civilians also fear the encroachment of the base on the city proper. See, for instance, Ian Dowdy, "Evaluating Encroachment Pressures on the Military Mission in the California Desert Region" (Sonoran Institute), sonoraninstitute.org/files/ProtectingCalDesertMilitary.pdf, accessed April 7, 2019.
19. Ibid. Urbanizing, developing, or unpaved areas near the base may instigate dust events that hinder training.
20. Three military installations along the US/Mexico border (Yuma Proving Ground, Fort Huachuca and Fort Bliss) have conducted significant air-quality investigations in recent years through the Strategic Environmental Research and Development Program (SERDP). Of the three sites, Fort Bliss has conducted the most studies. See SERDP, project map, map.serdp-estcp.org/index.html?Subprogram=air_quality/#, accessed April 7, 2019.
21. Echoing Ralph Alger Bagnold, a giant of geological physics.
22. Strategic Environmental Research and Development Program (SERDP), "Research Advancements to Reduce Fugitive Dust," www.serdp-estcp.org/News-and-Events/Blog/Research-Advancements-to-Reduce-Fugitive-Dust, accessed April 7, 2019.
23. Strategic Environmental Research and Development Program (SERDP), "Particulate Matter Emissions Factors for Dust from Unique Military Activities," www.serdp-estcp.org/Program-Areas/Resource-Conservation-and-Resiliency/Air-Quality/RC-1399/RC-1399, accessed April 7, 2019.
24. Jason P. Field, "The Ecology of Dust," *Frontiers in Ecology and the Environment, 8 (2010): 423–30.*
25. Gilles would argue that training produces only local particulate matter (PM) effects, not significant regional storms or on an annual time scale. See SERDP, "Characterizing and Quantifying Local and Regional Particulate Matter Emissions from DoD Installations," www.serdp-estcp.org/Program-Areas/Resource-Conservation-and-Resiliency/Air-Quality/RC-1191/RC-1191.
26. The US Army Corps of Engineers (USACE), through its ERCD Geotechnical and Structures Laboratory, has studied the impact of dust in both "combat and sustainment roles." US Army Natick Laboratories, *A Study of Windborne Sand.*
27. Ibid.
28. See, for example, the website of the Whole Building Design Guide; the "Department of Defense" page, www.wbdg.org/FFC/DoD/UFC/ufc_3_260_17_2004.pdf.
29. USArmy Corps of Engineers, *Use of Vegetation to Promote Capture of Fugitive Dust on US Army Installations* (September 30, 2011) www.wbdg.org/FFC/ARMYCOE/PWTB/pwtb_200_1_107.pdf.
30. "An avigation easement is a property right acquired from a landowner that grants the right to fly over the property; the right to cause noise, dust, etc." Beth E. Lachman, Anny Wong, and Susan A. Resetar, *The Thin Green Line: An Assessment of DoD's Readiness and Environmental Protection Initiative to Buffer Installation Encroachment* (Santa Monica: Rand, 2007).
31. This shift is due in large part to the DoD's emphasis since 2001 on counterinsurgency training and combined arms operations. This signals a distinct shift from the open terrain models of desert and jungle warfare.
32. US Dept of Transportation, *Road Dust Management and Future Needs, 2008 Conference Proceedings*, westerntransportationinstitute.org/wp-content/uploads/2017/02/Dust_Conference_Proceedings_05-04-09_combined.pdf, accessed Jun 30, 2019.
33. Chris Jones, "The Marine Corps Is Quietly Monitoring Sections of the US-Mexico Border to Stop Migrants and Drug Traffickers," *Marine Times*, September 13, 2018, www.marinecorpstimes.com/news/your-military/2018/09/13/the-marine-corps-is-quietly-monitoring-sections-of-the-us-mexico-border-to-stop-migrants-and-drug-traffickers/, accessed June 30, 2019.
34. Melynda Venegas, "Harsh El Paso Landscape Ideal for Middle East Deploment Training," *Borderzine*, February 21, 2018, borderzine.com/2018/02/harsh-el-paso-landscape-ideal-for-middle-east-deployment-training/#prettyPhoto.
35. Eric McDonald and Todd Caldwell, "Geochemical and Physical Characteristics of Vehicle Endurance and Dust Test Courses at US Army Yuma Proving Ground," Desert Research Institute, www.dri.edu/component/content/article/180-dridivisions dees-extended-research/3100-geochemical-and-physical-characteristics-of-vehicle-endurance-and-dust-test-courses-at-us-army-yuma-proving-ground.
36. Edwards Air Force Base, for example, is located near a dry lake in a land of extreme climate temperatures and occasional dust storms, characteristics that make the site an ideal physical environment for flight-test activities. See Dowdy, "Evaluating Encroachment Pressures."
37. Dusty tank trails accelerate the destruction of the vehicles that cross them. Frank Elswick, "Military Bases Rely on Stable, Dust-Controlled Surfaces," *Midwest* (blog), July 11, 2016, blog.midwestind.com/military-bases-rely-stable-dust-controlled-surfaces/.
38. YPG includes a 1,560-mile dust course. *Military Ground Vehicles & Equipment*, a pamphlet published by Donaldson, donaldsonaerospace-defense.com/library/files/documents/pdfs/F112255-Military-Ground-Vehicle-Equipment.pdf, accessed April 7, 2019.
39. Steven N. Bacon et al., "Desert Terrain Characterization of Landforms and Surface Materials Within Vehicle

Test Courses at US Army Yuma Proving Ground, USA," *Journal of Terramechanics* 45, no. 5 (October 2008): 167–68.
40. US Army Test and Evaluation Command, *Test Operation Procedure* (February 27, 2012), www.dtic.mil/dtic/tr/fulltext/u2/a557002.pdf.
41. Graham K. Dalldorf, Eric V. McDonald, Steven N. Bacon, and George Nikolich, "Testing and evaluation of a synthetic polymer for dust suppression in military applications," paper presented at the 2008 meeting of the Geological Society of America, Houston, TX, October 5, 2008.
42. Todd Caldwell et al., "The Performance and Sustainability of Vehicle Dust Courses for Military Testing," *Journal of Terramechanics* 45, no. 6 (December 2008): 213–21.
43. The Chevy Volt was tested at Muggins in 2010. "Trailing Dust Test for Volt Gives New Meaning to 'Three Yards and a Cloud of Dust,'" Chevrolet, June 15, 2010, media.gm.com/media/us/en/chevrolet/news.detail.html/content/Pages/news/us/en/2010/Jun/0615_voltdust.html, accessed April 7, 2019.
44. Caldwell, "Performance and Sustainability."
45. Mark Schauer, "Joint Light Tactical Vehicle Tested at YPG," *The Outpost* 67, no. 18 (Spetember 2017), www.yuma.army.mil/outpost/2017/18Sept2017.pdf, accessed June 30, 2019.
46. As in the testing facility managed by YPG's Meteorology and Simulation Division. See Katherine Kaliski, "Pa. Guard Aviators Practice 'Dust' Landings in Texas Desert," *US Army*, January 16, 2013, www.army.mil/article/94420/pa_guard_aviators_practice_dust_landings_in_texas_desert.
47. See Pacific Northwest National Laboratory, DUSTRAN website, dustran.pnnl.gov/.
48. Paul Kennard, "Dealing with Brown-Out," *HeliOps*, December 6, 2018, www.heliopsmag.com/dealing-with-brown-out, accessed June 30, 2019.
49. Kaliski, the US Army website; "Pa. Guard aviators practices 'dust' landings in Texas desert."
50. Although they increase dust locally for short periods of time.
51. Frank Colucci, "Desert Defense," *Rotor and Wing*, May 1, 2010, www.rotorandwing.com/2010/05/01/desert-defense/.
52. US Customs and Border Protection, "Supplemental Environmental Assessment: Operation Skywatch II," June 2004, www.dhs.gov/sites/default/files/publications/0111_-_bw1_foia_cbp_009292_009438.pdf.
53. A. C. Thompson, "Years Ago, the Border Patrol's Discipline System Was Denounced as 'Broken.' It's Still Not Fixed," *ProPublica*, June 20, 2019, www.propublica.org/article/border-patrol-discipline-system-was-denounced-as-broken-still-not-fixed.
54. See TRAKER, described in J. A. Gillies et al., *Characterizing and Quantifying Local and Regional Particulate Matter Emissions from Department of Defense Installations*, final report for SERDP Project CP-1191, 2005.
55. Nancy F. Crum, Mark Potter and Demosthenes Pappagianis, "Seroincidence of Coccidioidomycosis during Military Desert Training Exercises," *Journal of Clinical Microbiology* 42, no. 10 (October 2004): 4552–55, www.ncbi.nlm.nih.gov/pmc/articles/PMC522372/.
56. US Office of Personnel Management, "General Schedule Qualifications Standards," www.opm.gov/policy-data-oversight/classification-qualifications/general-schedule-qualification-standards/1800/customs-and-border-protection-interdiction-series-1881/.
57. Greg Moran, "Border Patrol Agents Say Tijuana River Pollution Is Making Them Sick, and Officials Want It Fixed," *Los Angeles Times*, March 6, 2018, www.latimes.com/local/lanow/la-me-border-patrol-pollution-20180306-story.html.
58. Chris Eger, "Details on the New G47 Confirmed by Glock," *Guns*, April 12, 2019, www.guns.com/news/2019/04/12/details-on-the-new-g47-confirmed-by-glock.
59. Sebastian Rotella, "Scientist Airs Plan to 'Dust' US Border," *Los Angeles Times*, August 26, 1994, www.latimes.com/archives/la-xpm-1994-08-26-mn-31356-story.html.
60. M. E. Kabay, "Security Applications for 'Smart Dust,'" *Network World*, August 23, 2005, www.networkworld.com/article/2313585/security-applications-for-smart-dust-.html.
61. US Training and Doctrine Command (TRADOC), "Volume 2: Air and Air Defense Systems," odin.tradoc.army.mil/mediawiki/index.php/Volume_2:_Air_and_Air_Defense_Systems, accessed June 30, 2019.
62. "The Powdery Promise of 'Smart Dust,'" *Homeland Security Today*, www.hstoday.us/subject-matter-areas/surveillance-protection-detection/the-powdery-promise-of-smart-dust/, accessed June 30, 2019.
63. Michael E. Miller, "Bandaged Feet, Bleeding Hands, Violent Coughs: The Caravan Takes Its Toll," *The Washington Post*, November 1, 2018, www.washingtonpost.com/world/the_americas/bandaged-feet-bleeding-hands-violent-coughs-the-caravan-takes-its-toll/2018/11/01/d0330d90-de09-11e8-b732-3c72cbf131f2_story.html.
64. Ed Pilkington and Edwin Delgado, "Under the Bridge: Migrants Held in El Paso Tell of Dust, Cold and Hunger," *The Guardian*, March 31, 2019, www.theguardian.com/us-news/2019/mar/31el-paso-border-bridge-migrants-trump-beto-orourke.
65. The appearance of US Department of Defense (DoD) visual information does not imply or constitute DoD endorsement.

CIUDAD JUÁREZ, CHIHUAHUA
SAMALAYUCA DUNE FIELDS, CHIHUAHUA

IWAN BAAN

106.48°, 106.89°

CIUDAD JUÁREZ, CHIHUAHUA

CIUDAD JUÁREZ, CHIHUAHUA

LINEA

CIUDAD JUÁREZ, CHIHUAHUA

106.48°

CIUDAD JUÁREZ, CHIHUAHUA

CIUDAD JUÁREZ, CHIHUAHUA

106.48°

CIUDAD JUÁREZ, CHIHUAHUA

CIUDAD JUÁREZ, CHIHUAHUA

CIUDAD JUÁREZ, CHIHUAHUA

106.48°

CIUDAD JUÁREZ, CHIHUAHUA

SAMALAYUCA DUNE FIELDS, CHIHUAHUA

106.89°

SAMALAYUCA DUNE FIELDS, CHIHUAHUA

SAMALAYUCA DUNE FIELDS, CHIHUAHUA

106.89°

THE STAGE THAT REMAINS

MIGUEL FERNÁNDEZ DE CASTRO
NATALIA MENDOZA

ESTADO DE SONORA, MÉXICO

112.33°

In Spanish, the word *frontera* almost exclusively refers to the precise line separating two nations; in contrast, the English word *frontier* can also designate the open space beyond civilization, the unexplored world and a horizon of conquest. *Frontera* suggests containment; *frontier*, overflowing. Nowhere is this subtle conceptual difference more fully present to experience than in the Mexico–US borderlands. Seen from the south, the line is a limit; seen from the north, a domain in potential expansion.

This basic linguistic difference is of course the expression of deeper divergences in the historical formation of national territories, as well as in the prevalent modes of producing landscapes. We will here argue that the expansive nature of the American frontier landscape is achieved through iconization, while the Mexican borderlands are characterized by the overpowering presence of indexes. Each of these semiotic modes conceals past and present violence in its own way: icons substitute dispossession and extermination with smooth and recognizable images, while indexes are the scattered traces of violence unaccounted for.

Iconic Erosion

The first film shot in Monument Valley was *The Vanishing American* by George B. Seitz, which premiered in 1925. One of its scenes shows General Kit Carson granting the reservation lands to the Navajo: "You shall live here in these canyons that you love, forever. Look! The very cliff bears your image," he says as he indicates a cliff that vaguely resembles an Indian profile. This is the first time in American cinema that the iconic geology of the West and the image of the Native himself are merged.

When this film was shot, no more than fifty years had passed since the Navajo had surrendered, and three decades earlier the Apaches were still waging battle.

"The very cliff bears your image....
We will help you to live as white men live. We will teach you to farm, to turn the desert into green fields. All this I promise you."

The Vanishing American, 1925. Courtesy Paramount Pictures.

The generation that directly dealt with the extermination was still alive when the cinema first began to use their lands as a stage set to mythologize the expansion into the West. Natives themselves were hired to participate in shows and fairs and were required to display their identity and perform the violence that had been inflicted upon them. The material traces of such violence, however, were quickly erased, and the incipient film industry rushed to substitute it with a seemingly innocent reenactment.

It is significant that *The Vanishing American* was Monument Valley's inaugural film. Its first chapter opens with a quote from Herbert Spencer, "throughout all past time there has been a ceaseless devouring of the weak by the strong," which serves as justification to represent indigenous history as a succession of "natural" conquests culminating with the arrival of the white man. The film provides a racist rationale for the extermination of the Natives, but it nevertheless mourns with nostalgia the lost indigenous world. The ultimate frontier landscape is inhabited by the ghosts of the vanishing Natives since its first appearance in cinema.

Monument Valley's iconic status was consolidated through cinematographic repetition, above all in the westerns of John Ford. In *Stagecoach* (1939), the monumental red pillars of eroded sandstone begin to transform into recognizable silhouettes. The long journey by the stagecoach of the title actually takes place in the circumscribed space of Monument Valley, the travelers crossing again and again the same places without this appearing to contradict the long days of diegetic time. It was precisely this disregard for geographic realism that allowed the landscape to become so iconic — that is, for the image to become independent from the place it was anchored in and to become a container for other forces. This also explains why John Ford was able to record a dozen different stories on the same stage without feeling

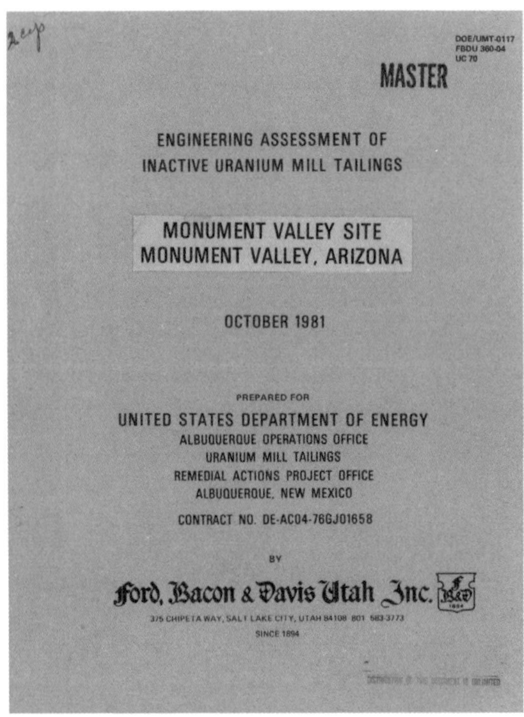

DOE/UMT-0117
FBDU 360-04
UC 70

MASTER

ENGINEERING ASSESSMENT OF
INACTIVE URANIUM MILL TAILINGS

MONUMENT VALLEY SITE
MONUMENT VALLEY, ARIZONA

OCTOBER 1981

PREPARED FOR

UNITED STATES DEPARTMENT OF ENERGY
ALBUQUERQUE OPERATIONS OFFICE
URANIUM MILL TAILINGS
REMEDIAL ACTIONS PROJECT OFFICE
ALBUQUERQUE, NEW MEXICO

CONTRACT NO. DE-AC04-76GJ01658

BY

Ford, Bacon & Davis Utah Inc.

375 CHIPETA WAY, SALT LAKE CITY, UTAH 84108 801 583-3773
SINCE 1894

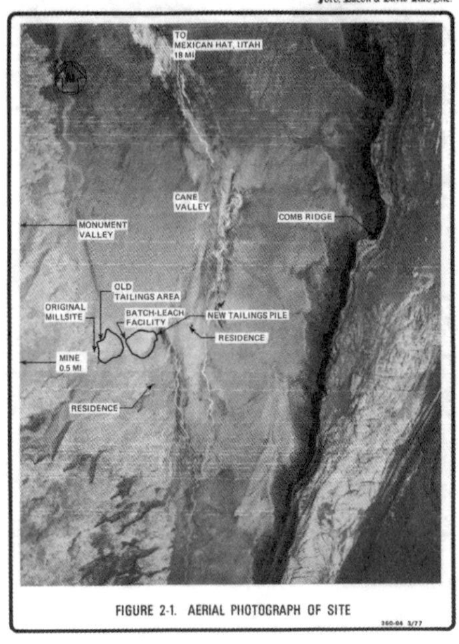

Ford, Bacon & Davis Utah Inc.

FIGURE 2-1. AERIAL PHOTOGRAPH OF SITE

360-04 3/77

2-8

Engineering assessment of inactive uranium mill tailings: Monument Valley Site, Monument Valley, Arizona, report, October 1, 1981; United States.

the need to change the location. As if by metonymy all the vastness of the West was already contained within this perimeter that in turn dilates; the fragment of a *meseta* seen from the limited interior of the stagecoach is enough to suggest the great expanse of the territory.

The iconic power of the landscape in the western cannot be disassociated from the threat it shelters: the Indian ambush. The walls of Monument Valley are not inert, but activated by the permanent possibility of a sudden attack. Unlike what would happen in an open plain, in this rocky landscape there is always an intermediate observer, the Indian, between the sky and the world of the whites. Within the logic of westerns, the Indian observer is already embodied in the landscape, blended into the sounds of the animals or sprouting from the peaks; and the ambush is therefore presented as if it were a natural disaster, a hurricane, or a dust storm, deprived of will and historical singularity.

The evocative power of the icon of the wilderness not only drains the native spiritual geography of the places it occupies, but also serves to conceal its status as a natural resource open to exploitation — in this case images engulf the material indexes of violence. Monument Valley has been used as the ultimate imperial frontier in two ways; first as the iconic landscape that made it possible to romanticize land dispossession, and then by supplying the uranium needed to consolidate the US as
a nuclear power and thus feed the fantasy of endless expansion. More than 500 uranium mines were in operation in the zone after 1942, and to date their waste has not been cleaned up. The Navajo miners worked exposed to radioactive material in poorly ventilated mines and carried the toxic dust home with them on their bodies. Supporting the military power of the United States meant, for them, that their own land poisoned them.

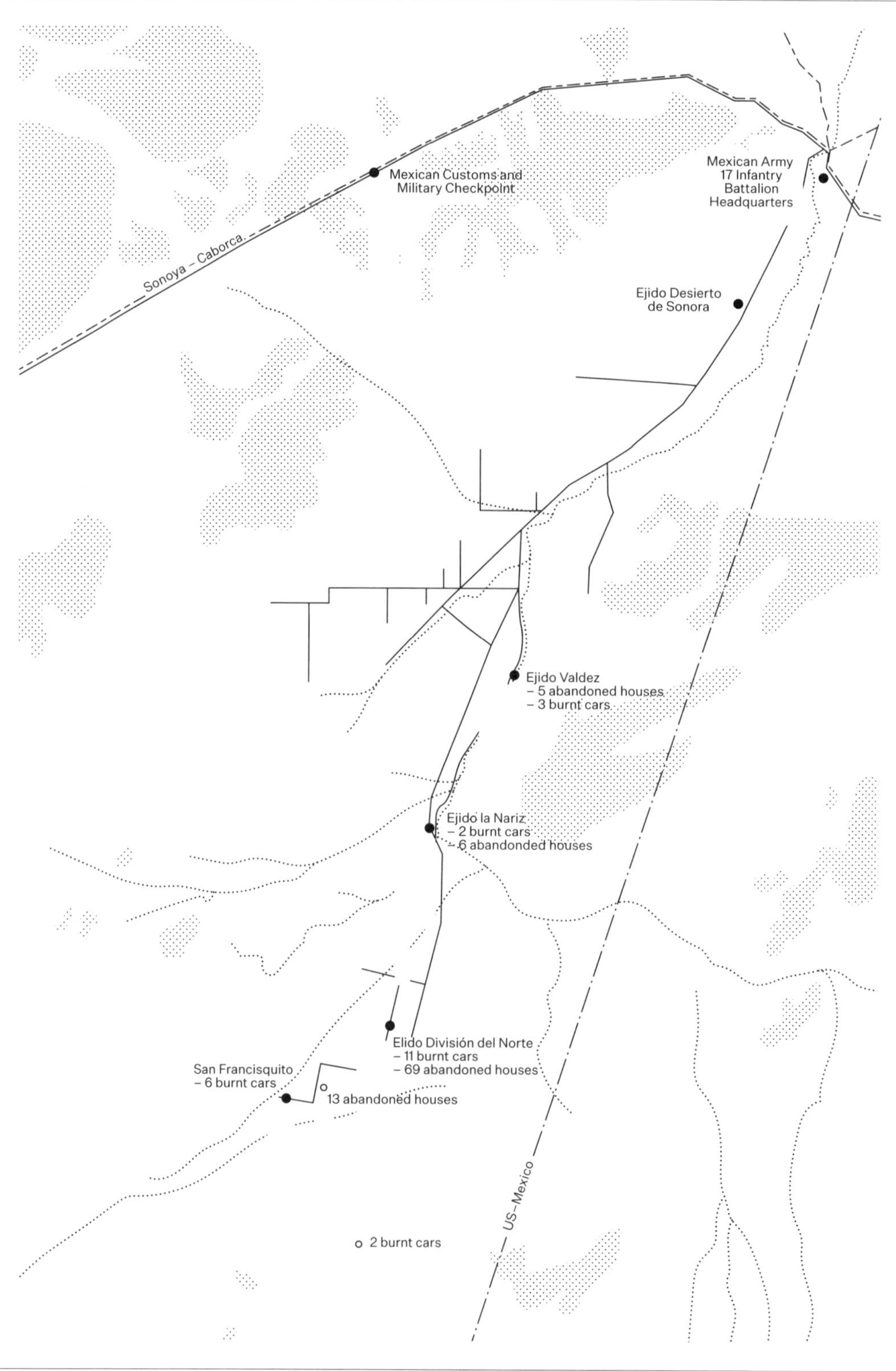
Mexican Customs and
Military Checkpoint
Sonoya – Caborca
Mexican Army
17 Infantry
Battalion
Headquarters
Ejido Desierto
de Sonora
Ejido Valdez
– 5 abandoned houses
– 3 burnt cars
Ejido la Nariz
– 2 burnt cars
– 6 abandonded houses
Elido División del Norte
– 11 burnt cars
– 69 abandoned houses
San Francisquito
– 6 burnt cars
13 abandoned houses
2 burnt cars
US–Mexico

Once established, the icon becomes portable. In the final scene of *2001: A Space Odyssey* (Kubrick, 1968), following the extraordinary voyage beyond the limits of the known universe, there suddenly appears the altered, yet familiar silhouettes of Monument Valley. The icon embodies open space in such a powerful way that after crossing galactic thresholds of pure light, we return to these terrestrial monoliths, as if in order to open up a new frontier it were necessary to carry with you the established image of the unexplored.

Indexical Disappearance

The reader should paint the line behind every scene of this story. It is the magnetic field that orients and rules all activities, the means and the end, the axis around which everything turns. Sometimes you see the actual border fence, but even if you do not, its presence is felt through the alertness of things and a distinct sense of finitude.

There is a small road that leaves Sonoyta and runs eastward parallel to the international border. It passes the headquarters of the Mexican Army 17 Infantry Battalion and meanders through fields and *ejidos*, small settlements of collectively owned land granted by the Mexican government in the 1970s. This dreary landscape is marked by vestiges of a long-gone agrarian enthusiasm, dusty warehouses with faded icons that read: "The new revolution is on the march. Society of Social Solidarity and Campesino Struggle."

Where the paved road ends, the nervous system begins: small trails multiply and take off in all directions, some lead to fields, some to settlements and some to the border itself. The further you advance, the more obvious the signs of abandonment. The last of the *ejidos* is called División del Norte, in honor of the revolutionary army of Francisco Villa, and has the same regular grid layout characteristic of modern state developments. But

Burnt cars at Ejido División del Norte, Sonora, 2017. © Miguel Fernández de Castro.

it is totally abandoned. The school is falling down, the windows broken, the benches covered in dust and the books scattered across the ground.

It is the same with each of the sixty houses in the *ejido*: a succession of broken fences, unfinished pillars, dried-out eucalyptus trees and broken-down doors with objects scattered indifferently before them. The hares move confidently among the ruins. Further on is the real battleground, a dozen cars burned and overturned, stripped down, with no tires. It all looks like an untouched crime scene. It is obvious from the position of the objects that the abandonment was hurried, but it could have occurred months or years ago; the material evidence of the violence is on show. All the erosion of the landscape leads to a single question: What happened here?

Contraband creates a particular type of territory and imposes an indexical reading of space, just like hunting or gold prospecting does. It demands a constant countersurveillance, deploying a network of *puntos* (watchmen) in strategic positions whose sole function is to observe and report suspicious signs: noises, traces, movements. There is a permanent sensation of being watched. The fact that everything here revolves around illegal economies intensifies the importance of the index because, unlike what happens in legal markets, you never see the commodity itself, only the traces of its circulation.

If you continue down the main road it is easy to miss a trail a little further on that breaks away to the south, leading to San Francisquito. The only signs of a settlement in this inhospitable landscape are a white water tank atop a metal tower in the distance and a sign reading: "Tohono O'odham Community, Respect Our Lands, San Francisquito, Sonora, Mexico." And suddenly the village, with its little white church made of thick walls and with a square of polished cement for a plaza;

Entrance to Cu:Wi I-gersk (San Francisquito), 2017. © Miguel Fernández de Castro.

Saint Francis's Church at Cu:Wi I-gersk, 2018. © Miguel Fernández de Castro.

around it, forming a kind of circle, a dozen houses and a small cemetery.

No one lives here either; the houses are silent, open, full of dust and broken objects. Fifteen kilometers to the north passes the border, and to the south 50 kilometers of rocky, barely visible trails lead to the highway. The rest is desert, split up into ranches of thousands of hectares watched over by a single cowboy. In the tense stillness, a woman slept in the shadow of an open roof. Her face looked like she'd been beaten. Beside her were two saddles, and on the wall of the corral a snakeskin was drying in the sun. The following year the woman and the saddles were gone, but the snakeskin remained in the same spot. Within the houses there were photographs and vinyl, dried oranges on the table, a cough medicine bought in the United States in the name of Dolores García Parra. The church door was open, and inside there were still images, petitions and fabric flowers, but the arrangement of objects around the altar marked the empty space where the venerated figure of San Francisco had disappeared. It had been taken to another chapel because there "the mafia had got really tough."

The line of the border between the United States and Mexico that resulted from the Gadsden Purchase of 1853 split the ancestral territory of the Tohono O'odham in half, and by way of compensation, three border crossings were established for their exclusive use. In Arizona, the O'odham founded one of the largest reservations in the United States; by contrast, the Mexican government converted their lands into national territory, which was opened up to colonization since they were not "duly exploited." The O'odham retained possession of a dozen ranches and settlements in Sonora and for a century continued to move freely across their lands between the two countries. In 1950, around fifty people lived in San Francisquito, and it is calculated that for the San Francisco's patronal feast some 200 people arrived in

House interior at Cu:Wi I-gersk, 2018. © Miguel Fernández de Castro.

carts and on horseback from Sonora and Arizona. Today most of their villages are empty and the border crossings are closed.

The dispossession and extermination of the Tohono O'odham in Mexico has been silent and invisible, despite the fact that all the signs are there to be seen. The brief newspaper articles that mention the violence in the *ejidos* of Sonoyta and the forced displacement of their inhabitants do not say a word about San Francisquito. The violence exercised in this territory escapes both icon and narrative; it is irremediably indexical. It presents itself as a field of loose clues that can hardly fit into a logical sequence or a general explanation of things. Violence is not accompanied by words, nor by ideological coverage. It is above all a violence without subject, the material manifestation of a hidden, illegal sphere that no one can adjudicate to themselves, and no one takes responsibility for. Forced disappearance is the emblematic form taken by this violence precisely because it leaves you with nothing but scattered traces.

The seemingly continuous appearance of the desert covering the Mexican North and the US Southwest can be misleading; even though the stage might seem the same, nature itself has been shaped materially and virtually in divergent ways. Landscapes are constituted by semiotic devices complicit with different forms of violence and domination. The more the Empire expands its horizon by relying on the iconization of nature, the more images in the lands beyond the line erode down to puzzling fragments.

Old photograph found on-site at Cu:Wi I-gersk, 2018. © Miguel Fernández de Castro.

TECATE, BAJA CALIFORNIA
TIJUANA, BAJA CALIFORNIA

IWAN BAAN

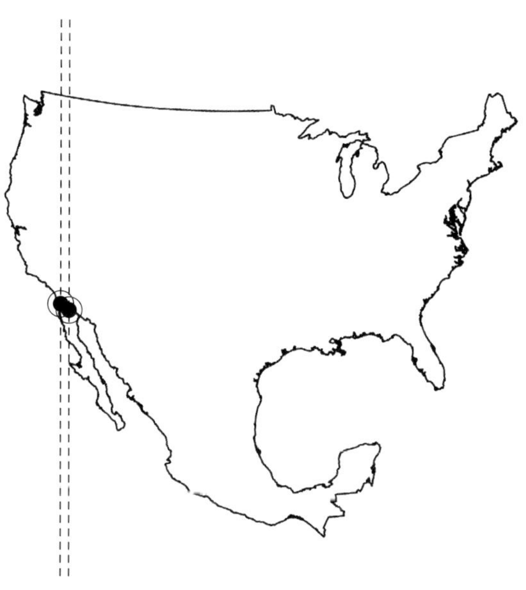

116.62°, 117.03°

TECATE, BAJA CALIFORNIA

116.62°

SE
USARA
GRUA
MONTE PIO
¡Acércate!
nosotros te ayudamos
654 6389
18.065
18.190

TECATE, BAJA CALIFORNIA

116.62°

TIJUANA, BAJA CALIFORNIA / SAN DIEGO, CALIFORNIA

TIJUANA, BAJA CALIFORNIA

TIJUANA, BAJA CALIFORNIA

TIJUANA, BAJA CALIFORNIA

TIJUANA, BAJA CALIFORNIA

TIJUANA, BAJA CALIFORNIA

117.03°

TIJUANA, BAJA CALIFORNIA

TIJUANA, BAJA CALIFORNIA

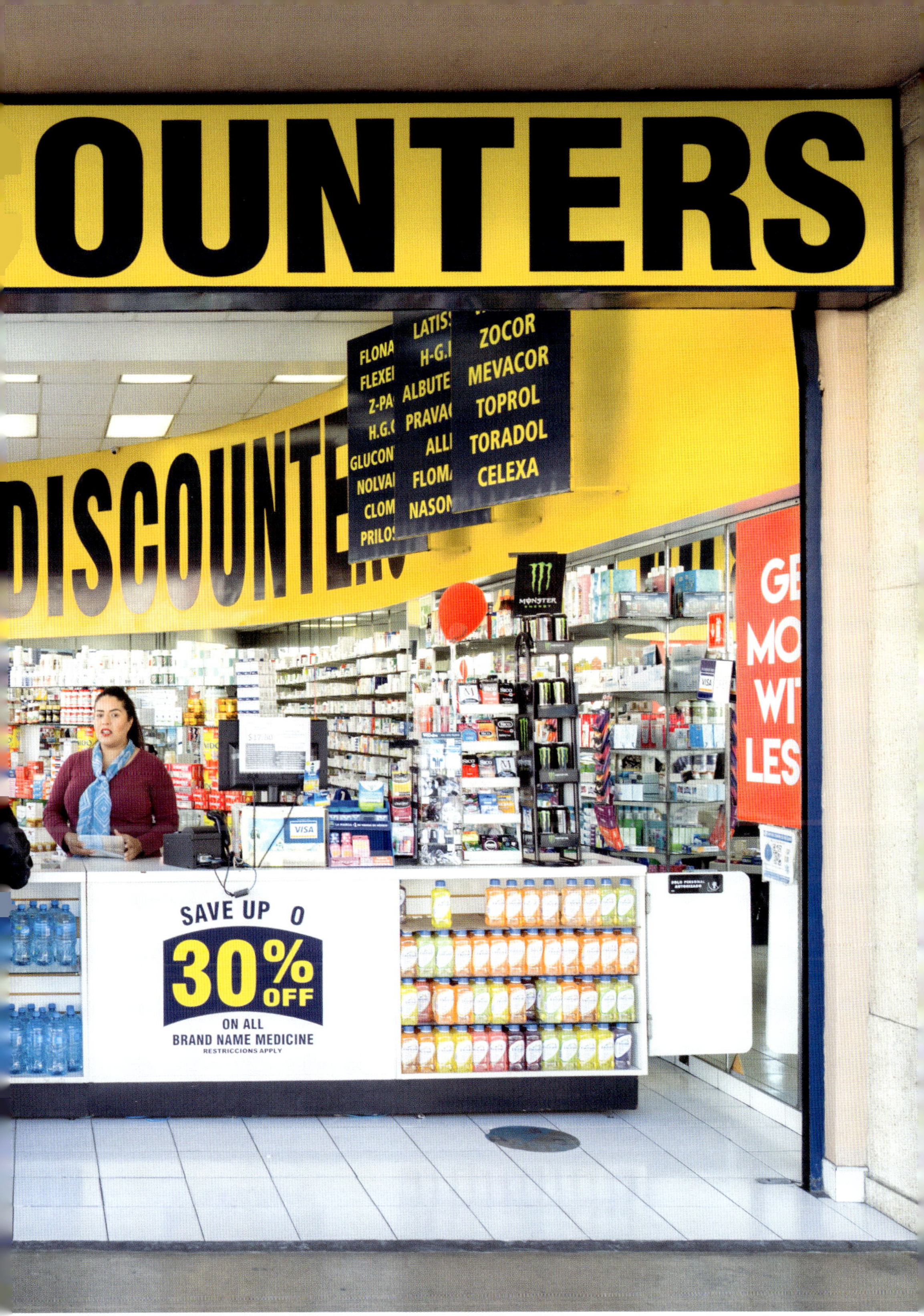

117.03°

TIJUANA, BAJA CALIFORNIA

PHARMACY
REVOLUCION

TIJUANA, BAJA CALIFORNIA

TIJUANA, BAJA CALIFORNIA

TIJUANA, BAJA CALIFORNIA

TIJUANA, BAJA CALIFORNIA

117.03°

DOUBLE AGENTS

CARLA FERNÁNDEZ
PEDRO REYES

TIJUANA, BAJA CALIFORNIA

117.03°

Weeks ago, the migrant caravan of Central American refugees known as the Viacrucis del Migrante attempted to cross into the United States through Tijuana. After walking 1,400 miles over many months, the men, women and children, many of them barefoot, were forced back at the Mexico–United States border by US military forces using tear gas and rubber bullets.

For the last two centuries the United States has conducted countless military interventions in Central America. To protect the business interests of North American fruit companies and maintain political control of the region, the US government has removed Central American political leaders not willing to follow orders; they have overthrown democratically elected governments as well as armed and trained counterinsurgency groups. It is a violent and destructive foreign policy that violates international human rights laws and has forced thousands of Central Americans to seek asylum elsewhere.

We initially had the idea of making a map to illustrate these US military interventions, but there were simply too many to fit on one page. We kept making the type smaller and smaller, but it became unreadable. We had to shorten the text and then split it into different historical periods just to give a glimpse of the uninterrupted cruelty suffered by Central Americans at the hands of the United States.

The result is these two maps, which highlight the moral and legal responsibility of care owed to these refugees by the United States.

If you can, put yourself in my shoes. Look at them: worn for hundreds and hundreds of miles crossing pebbled river beds, scorching hot sand, cold mountain tops; torn from thorns, sharp stones, and from running scared. These feet left everything that is familiar and dear to them: my wet homeland, the red earth that saw me take my first steps, and walk up the aisle– home.

Families walk an average of 1400 miles to the U.S. border every day—the same distance as 53 marathons, one day after the other—seeking asylum, fleeing life-threatening violent conditions back home, often resulting from U.S. backed gun violence. In exchange for their safety, they are willing to work the jobs no one else wants, for the lowest pay, and contribute to American society in countless ways.

Imagine my teddy bear, I like touching its little soft ear. We ran away together from El Salvador where my life was threatened. I am eight years old and I know how to pronounce these words: "my life has been threatened".

Three in five children leaving El Salvador are fleeing gang violence. Then, at the border, over 12,000 children have been systematically separated from their parents, a rate of 65 per day, while the parents remain in federal custody or are deported back without their children.

Imagine that time when you lost your mom at the supermarket. Remember? Imagine that instead of wandering away, someone snatched you from her arms, then forced you into a sort of jail with many other lost children. For months and months. I'm four years old, I can't tell the time but I know I'm not a criminal. Why am I being punished then? It feels like I will never see my mother again. Ever, ever.

On average children are separated from their parents for several days, up to over a year. According to the American Pediatric Association, this practice has caused "irreparable harm" and "permanent emotional harm" to the children.

Imagine waking up every day and not knowing if you'll come back to your children, if you'll smell their curly hair again, if you'll hold their sticky hands once more. Imagine running away from a life of fear, only to have your children taken away from you by strangers, speaking a language you don't understand.

On average, women are raped twice on their way to the U.S. border. This risk is preferable than what happens back home. Then, upon arrival, they are separated from their children, a cruel and unusual punishment.

Imagine an average-sized elementary school full of children; like yours, like me, but who have not seen their parents in months and live in inhumane conditions.

To this day, despite a court order, at least 416 children still remain detained in shelters, 14 of those are under the age of 5. Parents are often detained thousands of miles away from where their children are sent, making reunification inaccessible unless legal and financial help can be obtained.

Imagine seeing your baby boy and girl, after months of not holding them, to feel their heart beating against yours one more time, to see their smile; he lost a new tooth and you missed it; she learned a new word–survival–without you; they forgot how to sleep soundly at night.

The legal and humanitarian process of reuniting a mother with her children costs between $1,500 - $30,000 dollars. The damage done to the children is incalculable, to see them smile once more is absolutely priceless. With your help Immlgran T Famll IES Tog ETh Er has overseen 70 such families reunited.

Fifty percent of all sales generated from this collection of limited and special editions will be donated to Immigrant Families Together in an effort to reunite families who have been separated and who are now in detention centers in the United States.

The remaining 50% will be donated to Taller Flora AC, an organization which invests in workshops focused on design, quality and organizational development in artisanal communities of Mexico to support them in their economic autonomy and thus slow migration in search of better opportunities.
Please inquire if you are interested in making a special donation.

ABOUT
IMMIGRANT FAMILIES TOGETHER:

IFT is a national network of volunteers working to assist children and families impacted by US immigration policies that have led to the separation of families. Since June of 2018, we have mobilized hundreds of individuals across the country to pay the bonds of parents and young adults so that they may be released from immigration detention (52 as of November 2018). Further we have provided legal, medical, social support as well as transportation, food, clothing and shelter to hundreds of individuals nationwide. We work with established entities, individual attorneys and local and state government to help expedite reunification and provide support wherever needed.

IFT has grown to included hundreds of volunteers. We have raised over $1,000,000 bonding out 52 individuals out of immigration detention to be reunited with their children and families. We have overseen the reunifications of 70 families separated by current immigration policies, including the delayed release of unaccompanied minors to family members. Further we have supported their travel, legal, health, shelter, food and supplies and helped dozens of families across the country with acute effects of the administration's detainment of children. We have in some cases, assisted the reunification of children with their parents who had been deported. In addition to fundraising bonds,

IMMIGRANT FAMILIES TOGETHER:

- Provides government and foster agency-aproved housing when needed to expedite reunification
- Provides food and furnishings to families
- Provides transportation within the city
- Assists in obtaining lenient visitation rights and release of children held in foster care
- Assists in obtaining physical and mental health services for our families
- Secures additional funds required to comply with federal and state regulations for the release of children, when needed

ABOUT THE MAP:

At the time Europeans arrived to colonize the American continent, it was home to 77 million Indigenous inhabitants: 95% of them were killed and only 3.6 million survived. This is still the largest genocide in the history of the planet. In the past five hundred years, Native Peoples have lived as outcasts in their own land, a land they have inhabited for the last 11,000 years.

This map is a collaboration between Pedro Reyes and Carla Fernández. It attempts to show that our current political borders are used as a means to oppress and marginalize people whose human rights have been violated for generations.

As a graphic exercise, it is not intended to represent the official or legal boundaries of any Indigenous Nations or territories. For more accurate information we suggest visiting http://native-land.ca.

Family separation was used during the Indian Wars to destroy the Native American social fabric and remained active until the seventies. It is currently being used in Trump's administration's detention centers.
We denounce Donald Trump's crimes against humanity. We call for the abolition of ICE.

About Taller Flora A.C.
Taller Flora A.C. carries out training workshops in design, quality and organizational strengthening in rural artisanal Indigenous communities throughout Mexico. Our objective is to promote and rescue Indigenous Communities', ancestral techniques and supporting these communities so they can reinsert themselves into the economy by means of their trade. We believe that strengthening the economic autonomy of these communities, located principally in rural areas, directly impacts and lowers the migration and displacement of people who are forced to leave their communities due to lack of opportunities.

All t-shirts and prints at the stand are hand-screenprinted by F*ck la Migra, a screenprinting workshop started by Diego Miguel María, who was deported without his son and works every day to try to be reunited with him and to help other deportees in similar positions through fair-paid jobs and solidarity.

1853: U.S. forces land in
NICARAGUA during
political unrest. 1854: U.S.
naval forces bombard
NICARAGUA. 1855:
U.S. forces land
in URUGUAY,
PANAMA,
NICARAGUA, and
MEXICO. 1856: U.S. interventions
in the isthmus of PANAMA. 1898: The
Banana Wars, occupations, police actions, and interventions on the part of the U.S. in Central America and the Caribbean. 1901-1903: Interventions in Colombia's PANAMA province, Theodore Roosevelt
intervenes to assist Panamanian independence from COLOMBIA. 1900–1970: The U.S. tropical empire
overtook the western hemisphere. 1907: U.S. war ships take possession of the Fonseca Gulf. 1910: U.S. troops
impose puppet government in NICARAGUA. 1912: United Fruit Company begins operations in HONDURAS. 1918:
U.S. army lands in PANAMA to protect United Fruit plantations. 1920: GUATEMALA: U.S. sends armed forces
to ensure new president is amenable to U.S. corporate interests. 1926-1933: U.S. Marines occupy NICARA-
GUA and fight against nationalist forces. 1933: FDR announces "Good Neighbor Policy". 1934: Good
Neighbor Policy. 1934: U.S conducted military interventions in CUBA, PANAMA, HONDU-
RAS, NICARAGUA, MEXICO, HAITI, and the DOMINICAN REPUBLIC. 1947: The
United Fruit Company, as the largest employer and landowner in GUATEMA-
LA, lobbies the U.S. government for intervention. 1954: GUATEMALA's
"ten years of spring," the U.S. installs Carlos Castillo
Armas, whose authoritarian government rolls
back land reforms and cracks down on peasant
and workers' movements. Between 1954-1990,
more than 100,000 civilians were murdered
by the successive military regimes. 1954:
CIA overthrows constitutional government of Jacobo Arbenz in GUATEMA-
LA. 1957: U.S. high school students
in the PANAMA Canal Zone burn
a Panamanian flag, spark-
ing riots that kill and
injure more than 100
people. 1965: U.S.'s "direct
complicity" in GUATEMA-
LA war crimes compared
to the "methods of Heinrich
Himmler's extermination
squads." 1966: Somoza
Debayle makes René
Schick president.
During visit to the
U.S. Schick volun- teers NICARA-
GUA to serve as an U.S. military base for
invading CUBA. 1971: 7,000 civilians in GUATEMALA
"disappeared" under the government of U.S. backed
Carlos Arana, nicknamed "the butcher of Zacapa" for
his brutality. 1977: U.S. and
PANAMA sign a new treaty
providing for Panamanian
control of the canal.

United States Military Interventions in Central America, 1853–1977.

VUNTUT
KASKA-DENA
INUIT
DRAANJIK
GWICHYAA
HAIDA
INUVIALUIT
DEGUTH
TEETL'IT
TATSAOT'INE
TUNUNIRMIIUT
YUPIK
KITLINERMIIUT
TANANA
GITXSAN
TUTCHONE
ITIVIMIUT
NETSLINGMIUT
ATABASCANOS
TARRAMIUT
PAALLIRMIUT
GWICH'IN
KUTCHIN
SAHTU
SLAVEY
NIITSITAPI
SIKSIKA
HALMIUT
TLINGIT
DOGRIB
KASKA
SAKANI
INUIT
KWAKIUTS
KTUNAXA
ALGONQUIN
BLACK
BEAVER
CHIPPEWA
FEET
NUMAKAKI
CREE
NAKODA
DAKELH
NASKAPI
DUWAMISH
CROW
DAKOTA
MONTAGNAIS
ABENAKI
SUQUAMISH
NATION
LAKOTA
OJIBWE
SENECA
MOHICAN
SHASTA
PAIUTE
MODOC
SIOUX
CHEYENNE
HURON
LENAPE
OHLONE
MIWOK
NAVAJO
CHEROKEE
PATAYA
HOHOKAM
HOPI
MAIDU
OMAHA
CHUMASH
APACHE
OSAGE
QUAPAW
CONFEDERACION
ANASAZI
MOGOLLON
COMANCHE
HOPWELL
IROQUESA
PAIPAI
YAQUIS
WICHITA
CULTURAS DEL
MISISIPI
MAYAIMI
KILIWA
COCHIMI
HUICHOLES
KARANKAWA
APALACHEE
CALUSA
MONQUI
HUAVES
TLAXCALTECAS
CHOLES
KIKAPU
JEGA
GUAYCURA
TRIQUIS
CHICHIMECA
AIS
PERICHU
TOLTECA
TEOTIHUACANA
TARASCA
AZTECA
TOTONACA
NAZATECOS
OTOMIS
KIKAPUACHES
GUAYOS
GUANAJATABEYES
INNU
DINJII
KAINA
NAKAWE
AIVILINGMIUT
AKILINIRMIUT
MUSHKEGOWUK
IMUUN
AYAMUN
ESGIGIOAG
KASKA
DENA
SIQUINIRMIUT
QARNERMIUT
IGLULINGMIUT
AHIALMIUT
GESPEGEOAG
IYIYIW
IYIMIWIN
ONAMA
IYNU
L'NUK
OMUSHKEGO
NEHIRAMOWIN
HARVAQTUURMIUT
MONTAGNAIS
MOWIN
MOHAWK
SIKUMIUT
MI'KMAQ
HAUDENOSAUNEE

PIPILES
CHOLULTECAS
CARIBE
NGABE
PECH
CUNAS
AWA
WAYUU
JUPDA
TUPINAMBA
NUKAK
TIMOTOCUICA
TUPI
CHOCOES
TREMEMBE
CARAS
CARIBES
POTIGUARA
JIBAROS
CARIBES
TABAJARA
CHIBCHA
AKUNTSU
GIOTACAZ
CHIMU
KARAJA
CADUVEO
CAETE
TUPINAMBA
GÉ
MOCHE
INCAS
KANOE
KAYABI
WAI WAI
MAKU
TERENA
CHAVIN
NABEB
KAYABI
WAI WAI
TUPINIQUIM
PARACAS
NAZCA
PANO
ARAWAK
KAIWA
GUAJAJA
AIMORE
CHACOBO
TUPI
TEMIMINO
CALLAWAYA
GUARANI
CARIBES
TAMOIO
WARI
TIAHUANACO
URU
TUPINIQUIM
LULE
AYMARA
GUARANI
QUECHUA
ARAWAK
PILNGA
CHANGOS
GUARANI
ATACAMEÑO
OMAGUACA
COLLA
DIAGUITA
CHARRUA
COMECHINGON
CARIJO
MAPUCHE
ATACAMA
NCA
CHONOS
HET
QUERANDI
DIAGUITA
MAXACALI
TEHUELCHE
TIAHUANACO
CHARNIA
CHULUPI
KAWASHKAR
SELK'NAM
CHOROTE
XAVANTE
CADUVEO
GUNUNA
VAMANA
CHON
TOBA

There is nothing you can dominate as easily as a flat surface of a few square meters. . . . In politics as in science, when someone is said to "master" a question or to "dominate" a subject, you should normally look for the flat surface that enables mastery (a map, a list, a file. . .); and you will find it.
—Bruno Latour, *Visualisation and Cognition: Drawing Things Together*

According to tradition, when Romulus, the legendary first ruler of Rome, set about founding the city around 753 BC, he ceremonially yoked a cow and bull to a plough and dug a deep trench around the Palatine Hill to mark the alignment of the future city wall. This furrow, called the pomerium ("beyond the walls" in Latin), was understood by Romans to be the sacred boundary that separated Rome from the territory outside. Where gates into the city were to be located, Romulus raised and carried the plough over, creating a bridge over the pomerium and a connection between the two sides of the border. As one version of the story goes, Remus, Romulus's twin brother, came to Romulus at the pomerium and derided the inadequacy of this line in the dirt to protect his new city. Remus leaped across the pomerium to prove his point, and Romulus in anger struck him down, exclaiming, "So shall it be henceforth with every one who leaps over my walls."

We have arrived at a political moment in the United States when many, like Romulus, seem to be obsessed with the sanctity of the nation's geographical limits (or at least its southern limit) and with those who would dare leap across it. Recent major political careers, even of presidents, have been founded on the fear of those crossing the border illegally and what effect they have on our side of the border. These politicians argue that this abstract line dividing us from them must be made more palpable, more visible, more functional — with concrete and steel, with walls — in addition to reinforcing it with soldiers, drones, political policies and economic measures. The line of the border, no thicker than a sheet of steel, should be reinforced as fact. But how did we arrive at this seemingly precise line crossing the country?

Unlike Romulus, those who defined America's southern furrow in the middle of the nineteenth century did so with little or no direct knowledge of the borderlands. The scale of the New World made it impossible to mark the ground itself, so instead they inscribed (or at least described) a line on a map. This then-new border — defined in part as the centerline of the natural trench produced by the meandering Rio Grande, and in part by the east-west line of the 28th parallel north — was merely the latest in a series of unstable, abstract limits placed on maps by colonizers and their descendants as they volleyed for control of territory in the New World. As the border makes its way 1,954 miles (3,145 kilometers) from east to west, it crosses deserts, rough terrain, rivers and native lands; the map reduced this distance to a few inches, to a bold ink line, making it portable and pliable. It might be only a slight exaggeration to say that it was the map that enabled not only the border to exist, but the New World itself.

Maps, because of their visual accessibility, immediacy and vividness, played a key role in how we defined, and how we today visualize and understand, our identity as a nation. Simultaneously works of art and of technology, maps are hybrid objects embedded with the science and politics of their time. Maps not only reflect how we have understood the world but also define how we see the world. The seemingly neutral map of the United States that hangs on the wall of every sixth-grade classroom communicates ideological messages about the space of nation-states and the primacy of political borders over other kinds of geographic and cultural knowledge. From that map, each schoolchild understands borders as the highest level at which we sort the world, before natural features like mountains and oceans. The map conveys to them a sense of what part of the world they belong to, what part shares their values, what space is safe for them and therefore must be protected.

In 1492 maps did not yet play this role. Mapmaking as we understand it today originated in the Renaissance around the time of Europe's first contact with the new continents; and mapmaking's development accelerated precisely in parallel with the expansion of the known world and as part of the scientific revolution. Earlier medieval maps in Europe had often primarily represented abstract religious/ideological worldviews without geographic accuracy. The iconic T-O maps, for instance, were more like diagrams of a Christian world — they show Jerusalem as the center of a disc-shaped world, consisting of three geometrically regular continents. The earliest representations of America sent to Europe in the fifteenth and sixteenth centuries were not maps at all, but were written narrative accounts — journals and letters penned by Columbus, Cortez and others as they interacted and observed new lands and people, but these were quickly supplemented by visual representations.

The first maps that showed America were practical objects. Hand-ruled and painted in bright colors on vellum and calf skin, they illustrated how to navigate across the sea and access the New World in support of expanding global trade and commerce. Beginning in the fifteenth century, the portolans of mariners, such as the 1578 map of the West Coast produced by

Joannes Martines, counterposed the irregular, iconic shorelines of the continent (allowing identification of specific harbors by their shape) against arrays of arrow-straight rhumb lines — geometric lines of constant compass bearing at set angles that allowed navigation in straight lines across the sea in a world where longitude had yet to be perfected. The layer of technical geometry applied to these portolans illustrates the emergence of a globalized technical language requiring specialized knowledge to both produce and to read.

Maps quickly developed as a tool for Western explorers to record, condense and represent what they were seeing, which allowed them to communicate their findings in a convenient, portable, scalable and reproducible two-dimensional form — gradually displacing the terra incognita of the North American continent with increasingly detailed geographical knowledge. Maps became a preferred visual way to index the economic potentialities of the New World to monarchs in Europe (who would never set foot on these new lands across the sea). Maps functioned as proxy objects upon which a king could stake his claim, communicating to others his dominion over remote lands, people and resources. Geographic knowledge reflected in the accuracy of maps became a sign of dominion — knowing was owning. By the simple stroke of a pen on a map, a king could erect a virtual wall on territory thousands of miles away; and with a boldface annotation, he could declare a New Spain, New Holland, or New France.

As explorers and settlers penetrated the new continent from east and west, they filled in the details of the interior: rivers, lakes and mountains, native villages and routes, locations of new settlements and of course boundaries. As an iconic way of representing complex geographic and political relationships, maps provided a convenient way of collecting, sorting and displaying information that could be "written" collectively by groups of authors, easily incorporating and building on the work of others, and could be "read" quickly by groups of readers. Maps did not require total understanding to look complete — their graphic scalability meant that they could easily represent a small amount of information or could expand to represent more. Detailed annotations in italic hand described characteristics of geographic features and native people — or the mapmaker's assumptions when things were unknown. Elaborate title blocks prominently and boldly announced the map's subject along with the mapmaker and the patronage of kings or governments. Later as maps became more commercial, these inscriptions focused on the mapmaker and the place of publication.

With the widespread application of mechanical printing to maps beginning in the eighteenth century, maps became more readily available, not only to merchants, politicians and others, but also to mapmakers around the world. Unlike earlier hand-copied maps, accurate mechanical reproductions enabled mapmakers to easily compare, correct and incorporate the work of others. Maps could be read by speakers of different languages without translation; an international trade in maps developed with centers first in Europe and then in the Americas. The technical requirements of intaglio printing, which utilized mechanical engraving of graphic lines with a stylus on metal (usually copper) plates, encouraged standardization of graphic conventions, which circulated rapidly among global mapmakers. Monochrome maps, sometimes hand-tinted, became the standard.

Political conflicts between colonizing powers and the emergence of new independent nations on the American continent produced an explosion of maps beginning in the middle of the eighteenth century. This war of maps, whose primary purpose was to illustrate political boundaries, paralleled major conflicts like the French and Indian War, the American Revolutionary War and the Mexican War of Independence, as well as minor territorial disputes. The deceptively simple graphic technique of using colored regions to represent unified political territories dominates these maps (as in John Mitchell's 1755 Map of the British and French Dominions in North America). This literal color-washing of the paper suppressed the underlying histories, battles, conflicts and mass relocation of Native American peoples in favor of clear political messaging: this land is open for settlement. Seemingly precise lines denote borders between territories.

Our current, or perhaps perpetual, obsession with the southern border can be traced to the end of this period, the middle of the nineteenth century. The US–Mexico border as we know it today was established at the end of the Mexican-American War in the Treaty of Peace, Friendship, Limits and Settlements between the United States of America and the Mexican Republic, signed on February 2, 1848. The treaty ended a two-year war between the countries over territorial disputes in Texas, which had declared its own independence just a few years prior. The border was described in broad terms, and the 1847 Mapa de los Estados Unidos de Méjico, published in New York by John Disturnell, was used to negotiate the border and was appended to the final treaty. It would take the United States and Mexican Boundary Survey, a binational group of surveyors commissioned by both governments, the next seven years to determine the precise alignment of the border. They slowly moved across the difficult terrain, encountering hostile native tribes and settlers alike, extreme weather, hunger, thirst and fatigue as they attempted to reconcile the abstract language of the treaty and the line on the map with a much more complex reality on the ground.

As maps of North America have continued to evolve and proliferate since the middle of the nineteenth century, utilizing more sophisticated remote imaging technologies, they have revealed ever more complex geographies and relationships. But somehow the complexity that sits just beneath the US–Mexico border today remains terra incognita. This border is the world's most crossed national boundary — in both directions — for people, goods and money, making it not an edge, as five centuries of maps ask us to conclude, but instead the center of a vibrant, interconnected Mexican-American region, which spreads across the continent, comprising overlapping histories, cultures, economies and natural systems. But the maps that dominate our thinking about the United States and Mexico rehearse the same familiar concerns with the mark on the page, delimiting one colored territory from another, continually reinscribing the difference between pink and yellow.

Over the last 500 years, maps have enabled kings, colonizers, settlers, governments, armies, and traders to understand, evaluate, visualize, and eventually dominate and domesticate systems and territories of North America with ever-increasing levels of sophistication. Although it is by now cliché to say, we are at a moment when globalized systems no longer obey national boundaries. Systems like the Internet instantaneously connect everyone, everywhere; businesses shift money and manufacture from continent to continent outside of the conventional boundaries of national laws; world financial markets have become totally interdependent; and existential threats like climate change impact all of us. The attempt to fortify an arbitrary line in the sand with some concrete and steel seems like little more than nostalgia when all these systems cross borders without even slowing down.

Studying the many historical and contemporary maps we have (some of which are reproduced in this volume) can give us clues about why we see the world the way we do and tell us something about where we came from. But the unprecedented conditions that bind us together across borders today necessitate the development of new forms of visualization and mapmaking. We must invent new graphic techniques to support a more radical cartography, unbounded by persistent colonial mapmaking ideologies and conventions, in order to reveal our shared connections, rather than our divisions. Our understanding of the world is already in transition as our awareness of the environment continues to deepen — new maps and models have emerged that represent the world in terms of ecologies. But we must extend this kind of ecological thinking to other systems as well — we must reindex our relationships to one other around shared resources and systems rather than around political ideologies. New maps must make the overlapping communities and regions created around things like watersheds, trade systems, infrastructures and diseases and their relationship to one another more apparent, allowing us to understand the world in more than pink and yellow terms.

US/MEXICO WESTERN BEACH BORDER

TIJUANA INTERNATIONAL AIRPORT

INSTITUTO NACIONAL DE MIGRACIÓN

NEW MEXICO/CHIHUAHUA CORNER BORDER

UNION GANADERA CIUDAD JUÁREZ

SOMEWHERE ON THE RIO GRANDE

PUENTE INTERNACIONAL PRESA LA AMISTAD

SOMEWHERE ON THE RIO GRANDE

RIVER BEND ON THE RIO GRANDE

MASSEY'S GUN SHOP AND RANGE

FORT BROWN MEMORIAL GOLF COURSE

SAN YSIDRO PORT OF ENTRY

US/MEXICO EASTERN BEACH BORDER

PHYSICAL FEATURES

INFRASTRUCTURE

LAND COVER

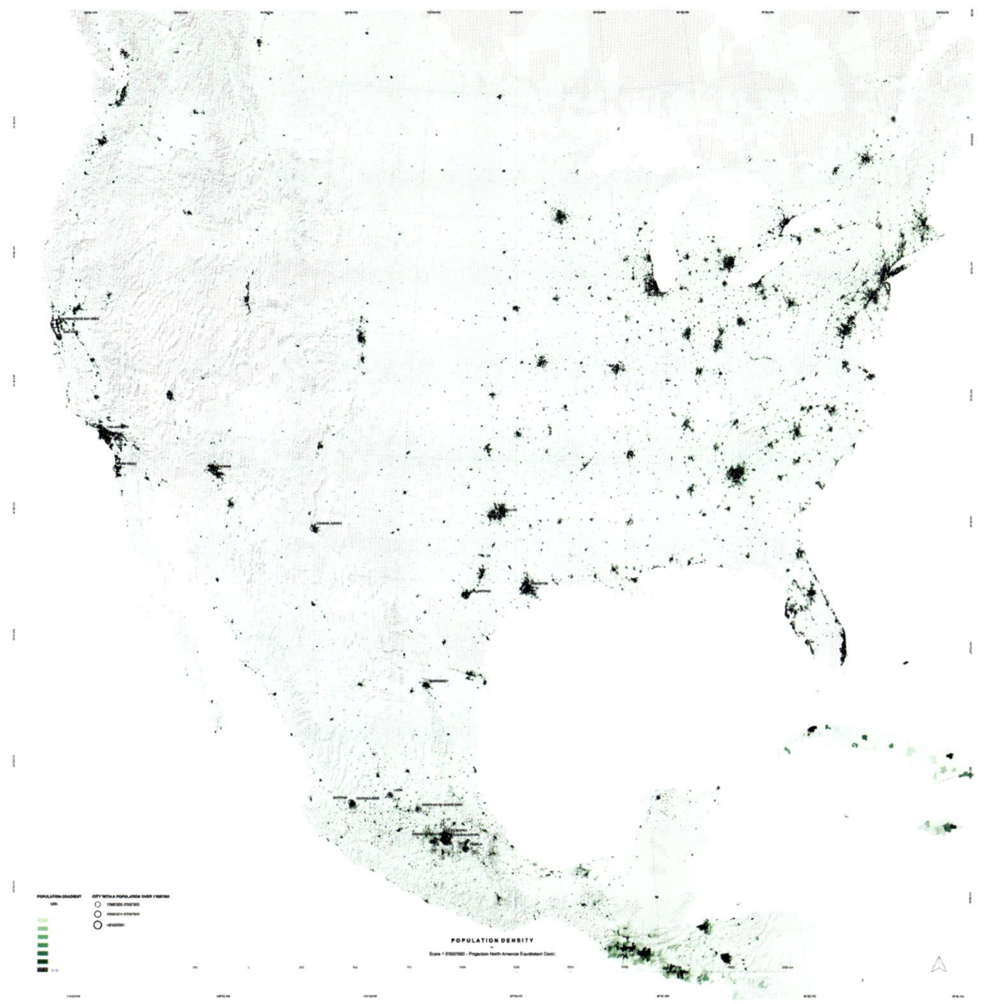

POPULATION

INFRASTRUCTURE

LANDSCAPE

MAPA DE LOS ESTADOS UNIDOS DE MÉJICO, 1847.
COURTESY LIBRARY OF CONGRESS.

MAPA
de los
ESTADOS UNIDOS
DE
MÉJICO,
LO PUBLICAN J. DISTURNELL, 102 BROADWAY
(NUEVA YORK.)
1847.
REVISED EDITION
GEORGIA
FLORIDA
BAHAMA
DE MÉJICO
ISLA DE CUBA
JAMAICA
BAHIA DE HONDURAS
MOSQUITO COAST

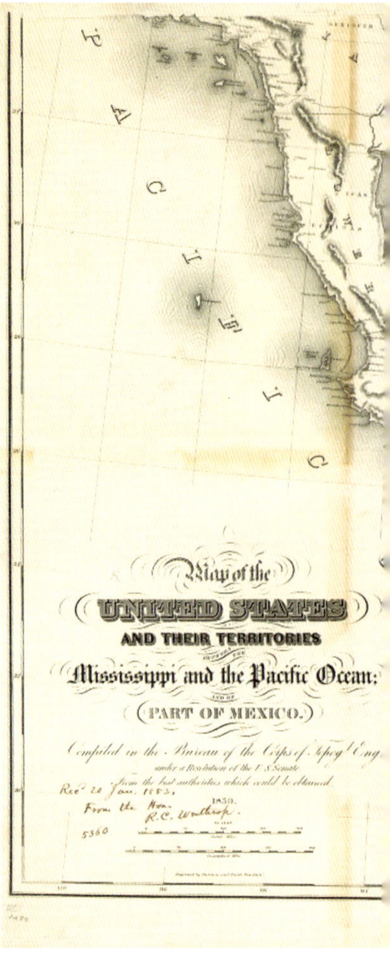

RELIEF MAP OF NORTH AMERICA, 1912.
COURTESY LIBRARY OF CONGRESS.

MAP OF THE UNITED STATES AND THEIR TERRITORIES, 1850.
COURTESY NEW YORK PUBLIC LIBRARY.

A HANDBOOK OF MEXICO: RAILWAYS, 1919.
COURTESY UNIVERSITY OF TEXAS LIBRARIES.

THE KINO PASSAGE TO CALIFORNIA, 1731.
COURTESY UNIVERSITY OF TEXAS LIBRARIES.

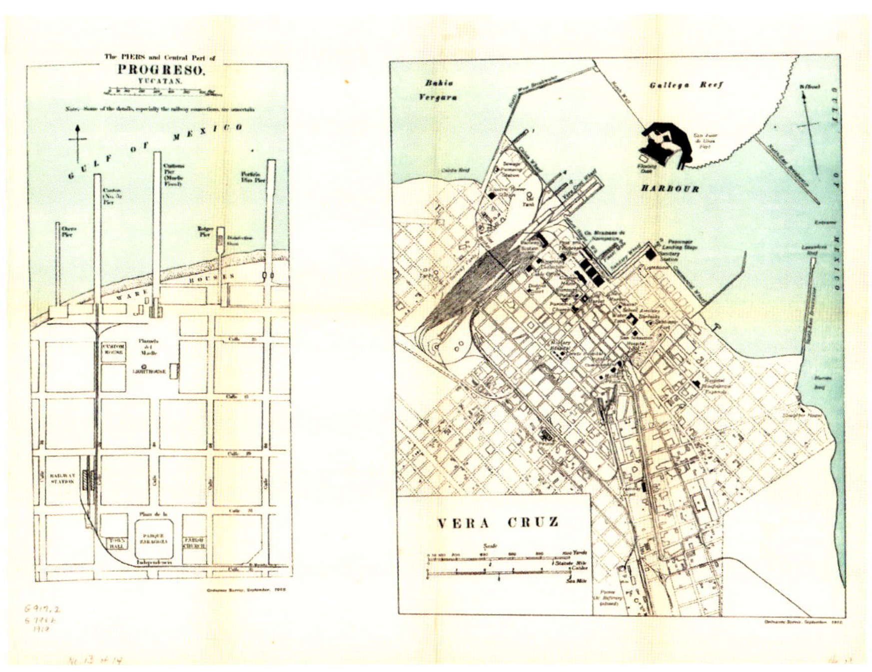

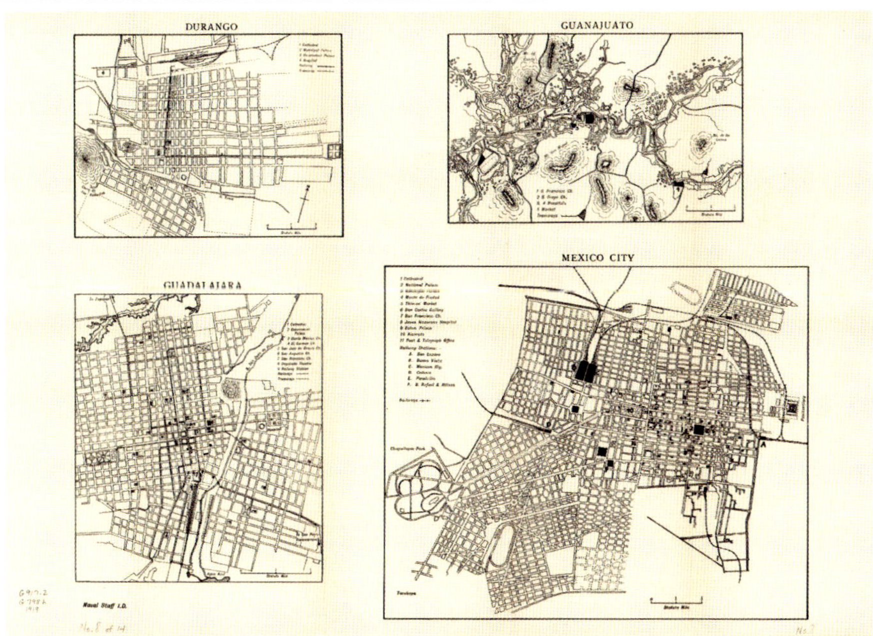

PLANS OF SEAPORT TOWNS: PROGRESO AND VERA CRUZ.
COURTESY UNIVERSITY OF TEXAS LIBRARIES.

PLANS OF INLAND TOWNS: DURANGO, GUADALAJARA, GUANAJUATO, MEXICO CITY.
COURTESY UNIVERSITY OF TEXAS LIBRARIES.

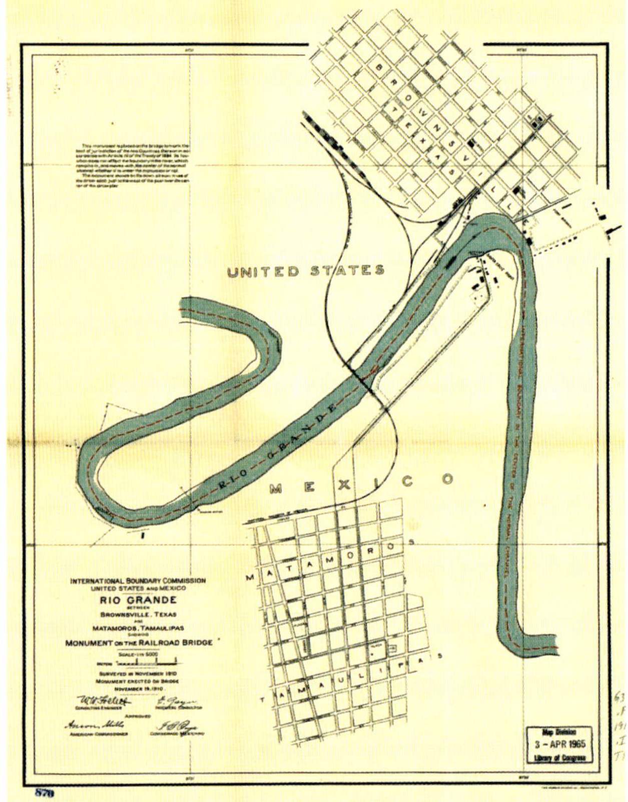

PANORAMA OF THE SEAT OF WAR, BIRD'S-EYE VIEW, 1861.
COURTESY LIBRARY OF CONGRESS.

BOUNDARIES BETWEEN BROWNSVILLE, TEXAS, AND MATAMOROS, TAMAULIPAS, 1910.
COURTESY LIBRARY OF CONGRESS.

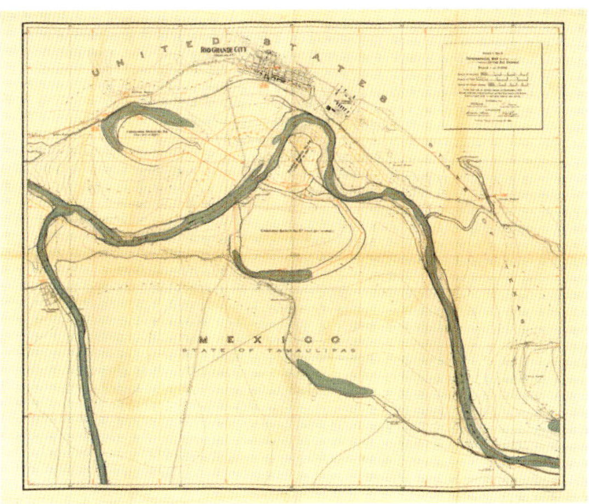

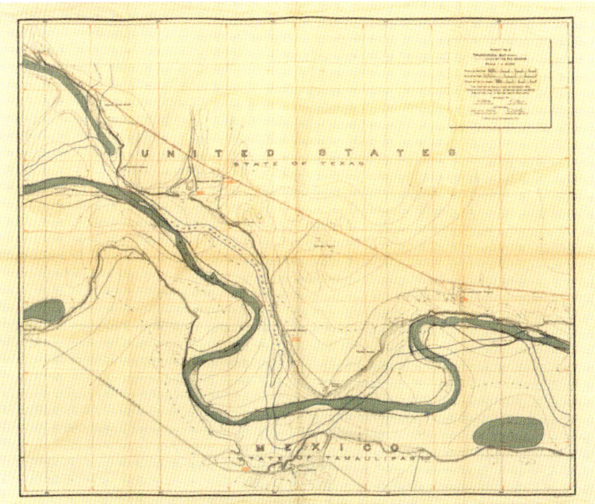

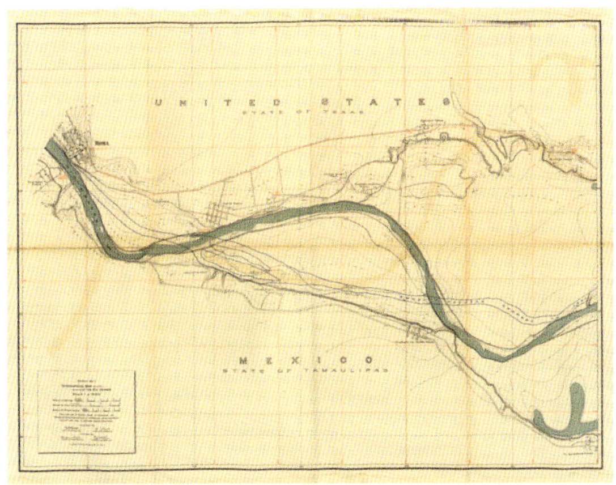

MAPS FROM THE SURVEY OF THE RIO GRANDE, 1912.
COURTESY UNIVERSITY OF TEXAS LIBRARIES.

THE RANGE AND RANCH CATTLE AREA OF THE UNITED STATES AND MEXICO, 1884.
COURTESY LIBRARY OF CONGRESS.

MAP OF THE UNITED STATES AND MEXICO, 1846.
COURTESY LIBRARY OF CONGRESS.

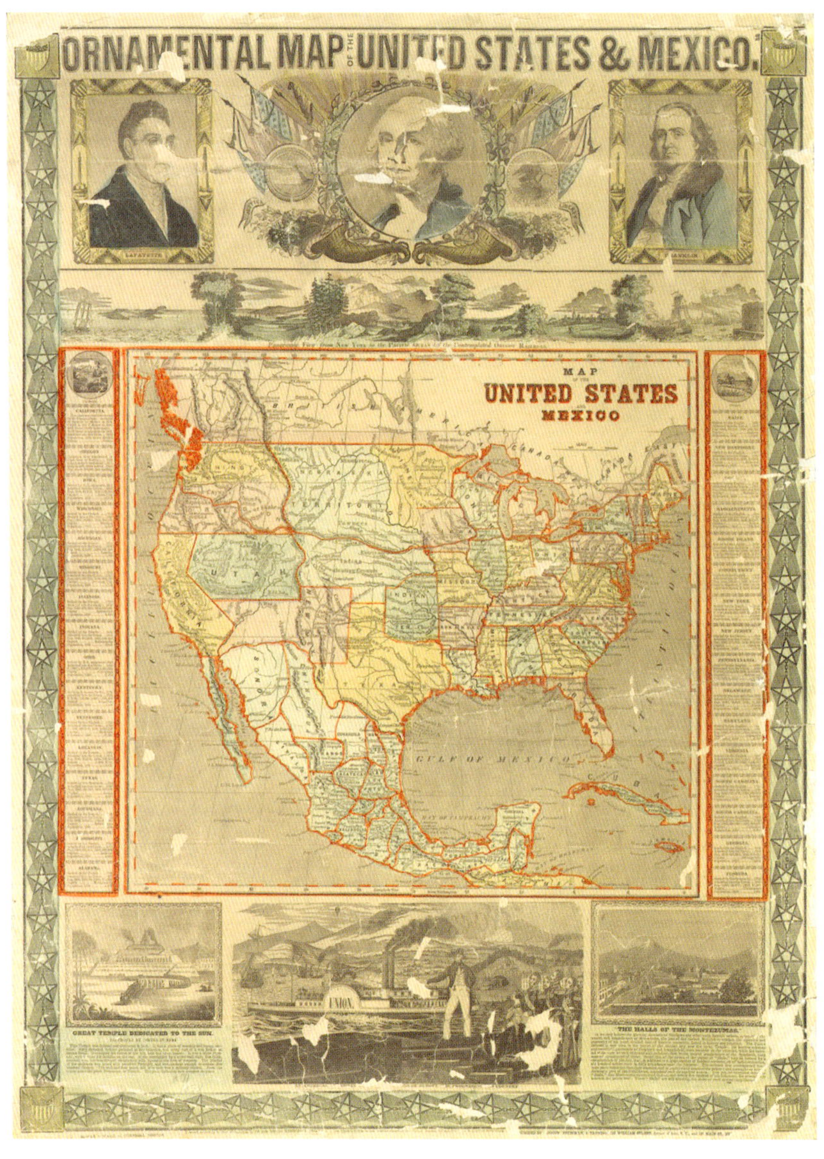

ORNAMENTAL MAP OF THE UNITED STATES AND MEXICO, 1847.
COURTESY BEINECKE LIBRARY, YALE UNIVERSITY.

NORTH AMERICA, 1844 G3.
COURTESY BEINECKE LIBRARY, YALE UNIVERSITY.

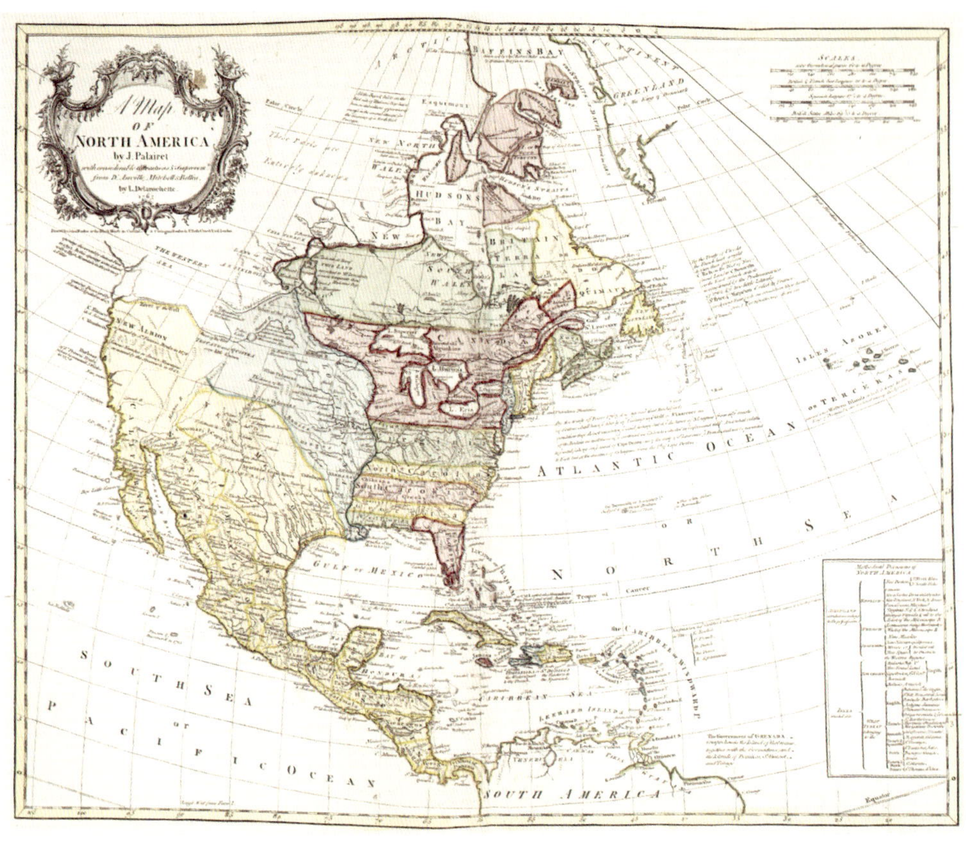

A MAP OF NORTH AMERICA, 1765.
COURTESY BEINECKE LIBRARY, YALE UNIVERSITY.

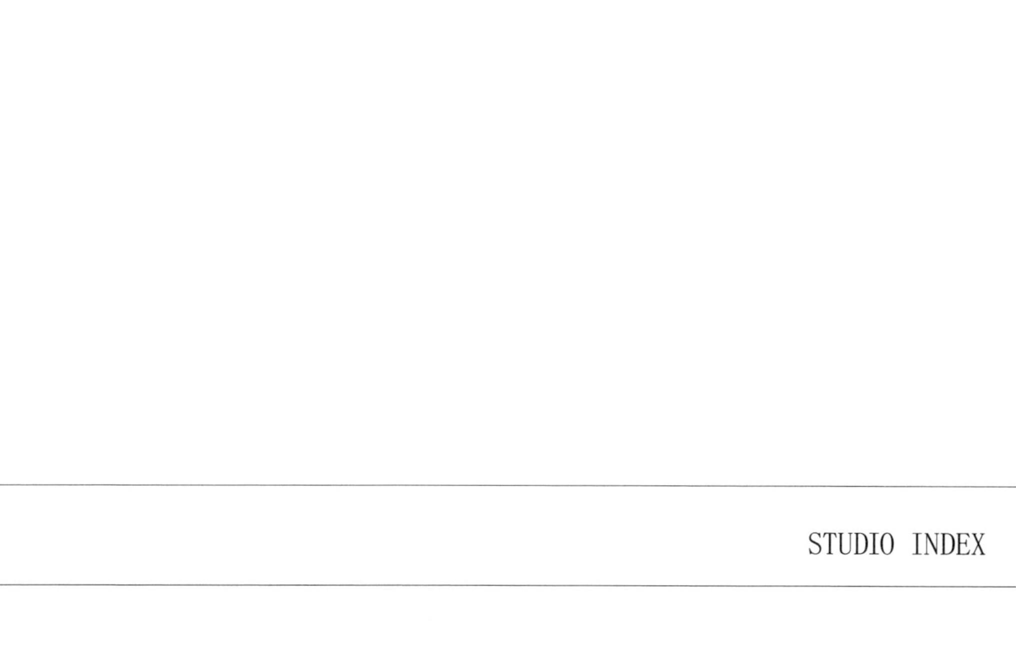
STUDIO INDEX

The Border

The Border is at the center of the debate in the United States. Despite living in the advantages of a globalized world, divisive lines between countries are on the rise. Politics in the United States revolves around building a physical barrier on the Mexico-US border region whose borderline shifted for nearly 100 years before settling where it currently sits on a map in 1848. Despite living in the advantages of a globalized world, divisive lines between countries and animosity between nationalities are on the rise. Politics in the United States revolve around building a physical barrier on the Mexico–US border, a region whose borderline shifted for nearly 100 years before settling where it currently sits on a map in 1848. The topic is a hotbed of political divisiveness — a violent line exclusion that this year led to the longest government shutdown in United States history. Xenophobic rhetoric is justified and embedded in this exaggerated border line which divides, but life along the border is instead divided by an inequality of infrastructure, economy and environmental systems. Even at the microdivisions at the border, the shared economies, values and culture overpower the inequitable divisions.

The student works at the border propose utopian futuristic and speculative projects in which the border region is a connective zone. "Fly on the Wall," a studio taught at Cornell University by Derek Dellekamp and Rozana Montiel, envisions border utopias enacted through long-range economic initiatives, multinarrative books and wood block stamps. In Raveevarn Choksombatchai's studio taught at UC Berkeley, border conditions are expanded and converted into shared infrastructure zones. Ersela Kripa and Stephen Mueller of Texas Tech University, El Paso, and Kathy Velikov of the University of Michigan each engaged in studios in the El Paso/Ciudad Juárez region. Kripa's proposals revolve around the shared air, Mueller's around the movement of dirt and dust and Velikov's on the complex politics of water. Through the exclusive physical barriers, oppression and violence of this border these proposals imagine a zone that could be mutually productive by generating jobs or increasing cross-cultural exchanges.

TWO SIDES OF A COIN

LOCATION: Tecate/Tijuana DESIGNER(s): Ellen Park, Yue Ma INSTITUTION: Cornell DESCRIPTION: The juxtaposition of images reveals a new narrative on the economic realities and delusions between two countries.

BORDER POLICY: EXTRA-STATECRAFT AND THE ECONOMICON

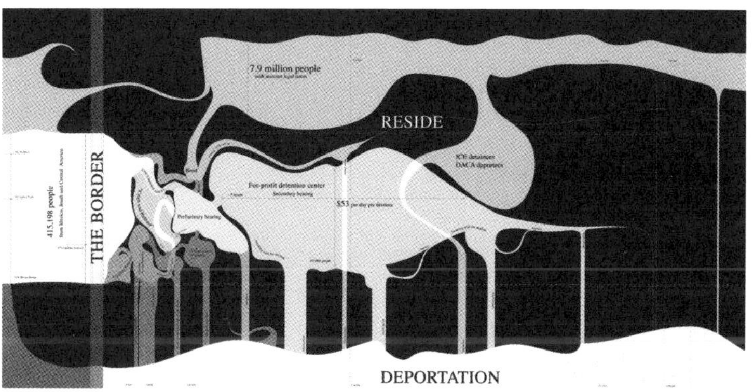

LOCATION: Tecate/Tijuana DESIGNER(s): Hallie Black INSTITUTION: Cornell DESCRIPTION: By examining US-Mexico border policy, the architectural implications of mass transference of goods, human or otherwise, arises.

CONTEXT

LOCATION: Tecate/Tijuana DESIGNER(s): Hyojin Lee, Kaylin Park INSTITUTION: Cornell DESCRIPTION: Like a series of lenses, a border is examined by its various geopolitical contexts: hypocritical, delightful, or dread-inducing.

ECONOMY: 2020, 2050, 2070

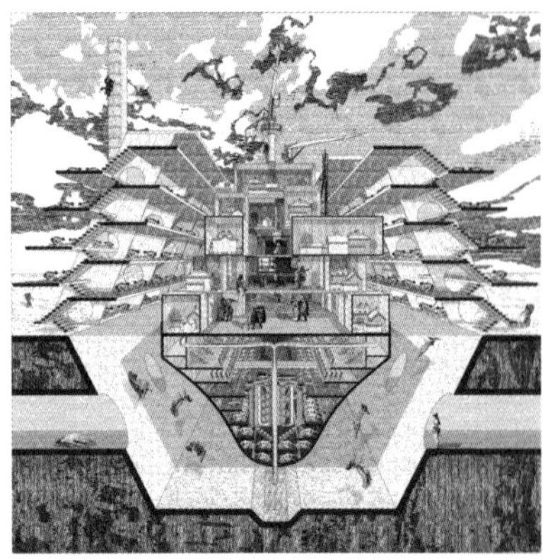

LOCATION: Tecate/Tijuana DESIGNER(s): Yue Ma INSTITUTION: Cornell DESCRIPTION: GDP and international cash flow rise within the border's no-man's-land—enchanting a new future with an autonomous, fortified vessel wedged between.

WILL TOWER

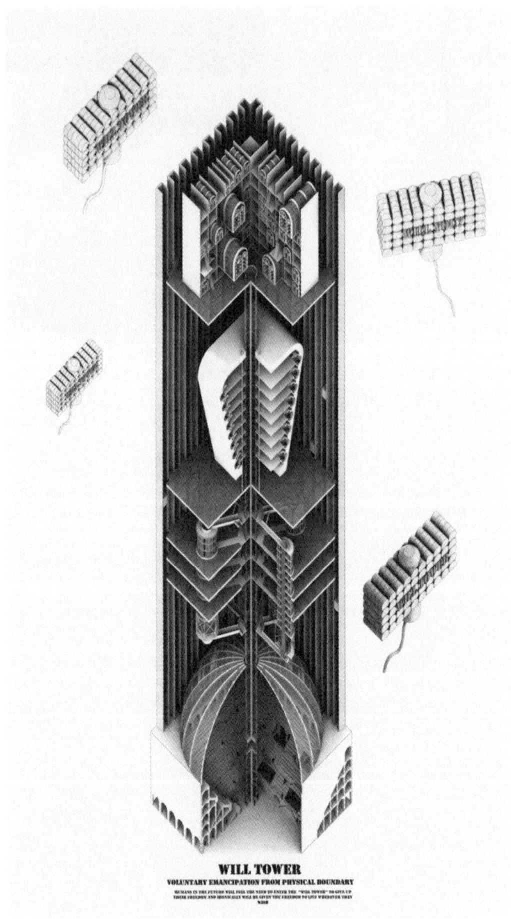

LOCATION: Tecate/Tijuana DESIGNER(s): Kaylin Park INSTITUTION: Cornell DESCRIPTION: The Will Tower grants peace or paranoia to the human capital that flows through physical and digital space.

ECOTONIC CITY

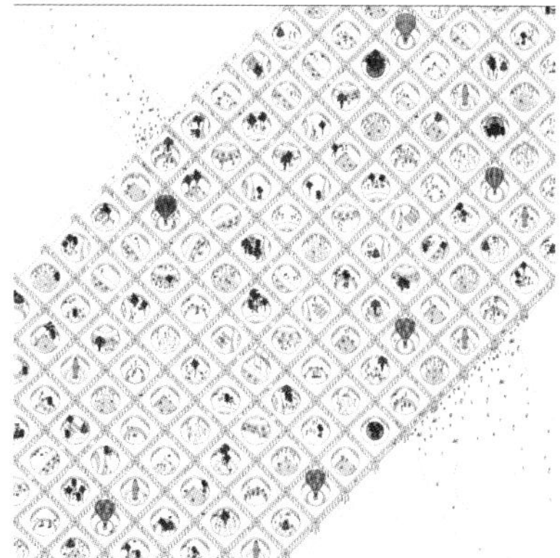

LOCATION: Tecate/Tijuana DESIGNER(s): Ellen Park INSTITUTION: Cornell DESCRIPTION: The physical ecotone between north and south sparks innovation for collaboration and newfound possibilities that cannot exist without the its other.

LAND USE REIMAGINING

LOCATION: Tecate/Tijuana DESIGNER(s): Drishya Chhetri, Siamak Saadati INSTITUTION: Berkeley DESCRIPTION: This project explores a design process that physically acts upon the surface of the landscape in search of design possibilities to create an expansive liminal space along the border between the US and Mexico.

THE CONVEYOR CITY

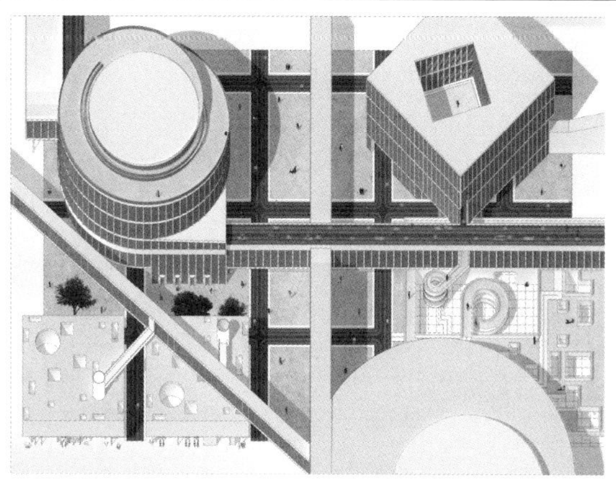

LOCATION: Tecate/Tijuana DESIGNER(s): Felix Yiu, Parama Suteja INSTITUTION: Berkeley DESCRIPTION: This proposal forecasts a city of an infinitely expanding border zone with a network of conveyor belts.

THE LAND OF SHADOW

LOCATION: Tecate/Tijuana DESIGNER(s): Kevin Aviles, Aboubacar Komara INSTITUTION: Berkeley DESCRIPTION: Shadows are explored as a conceptual design strategy to create safe and apolitical spaces within highly politically charged region.

TRANSPARENCY IN TRANSITION

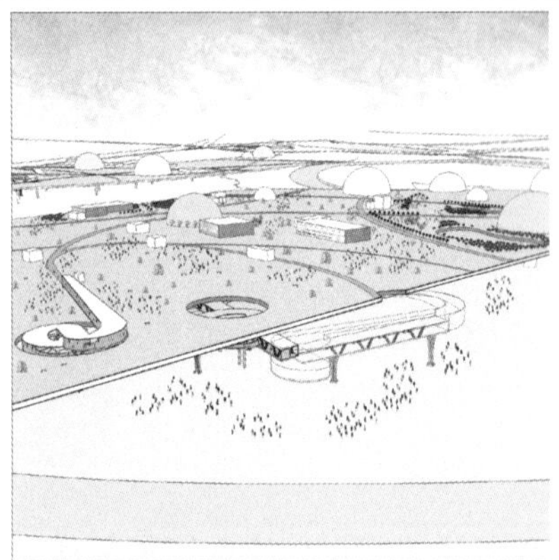

LOCATION: Tecate/Tijuana DESIGNER(s): Matt Giles, Hao Wang INSTITUTION: Berkeley DESCRIPTION: This project aims to bridge two warring sides of political tension through radical provocation from its camouflage form at a distance to an open and distinct landscape at human scale.

PILGRIMAGE THROUGH THE STARS OF OUR PAST

LOCATION: Tecate/Tijuana DESIGNER(s): Paola Noemi Gutierrez INSTITUTION: Berkeley DESCRIPTION: Located in the desert between Arizona and Mexico, this project intends to provide a liminal space where people can acknowledge and celebrate the evidence of divisiveness in ourselves.

REIMAGINING THE RIVER BORDER: LAYERED PERMEABILITY

LOCATION: Tecate/Tijuana DESIGNER(s): Tiange Wang, Margaret Zhou INSTITUTION: Berkeley DESCRIPTION: The superimposition of politics and nature inspires this project—creating opportunities and bases for agrarian, infrastructural and experiential accession.

BINATIONAL CURING CENTER

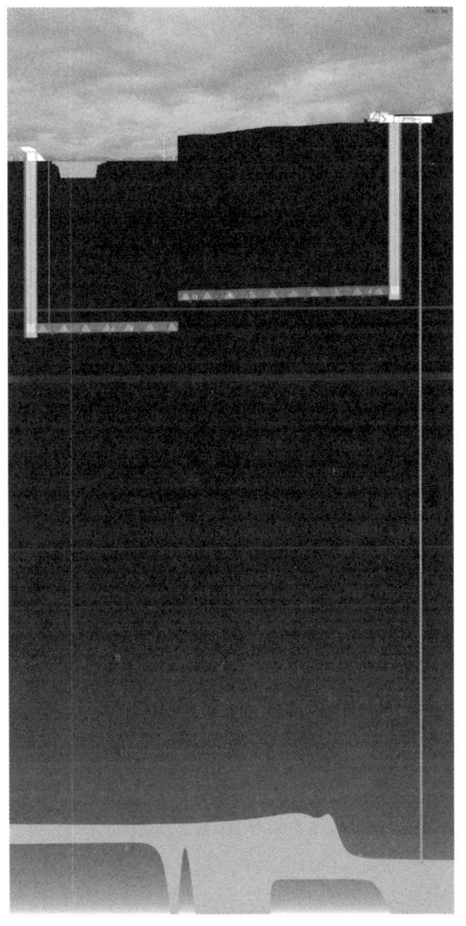

LOCATION: El Paso and Ciudad Juárez DESIGNER(s): Alexandra Cortez INSTITUTION: Texas Tech DESCRIPTION: Border space as catalyst for asymmetrical pollution policy and control.

WATER BUBBLE

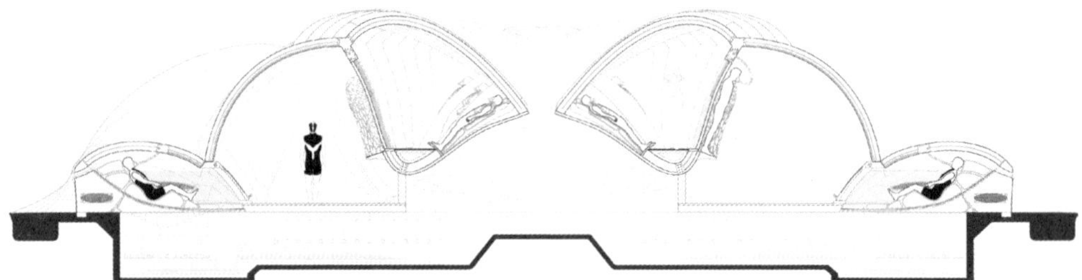

LOCATION: El Paso and Ciudad Juárez DESIGNER(s): Daniel Rios INSTITUTION: Texas Tech DESCRIPTION: Occupying binational water fluctuations of the Rio Grande. The project takes direct advantage of the binational politics of water control of the Rio Grande, using its fluctuations in order to power a mechanical system that regulates water baths for the treatment of respiratory disease.

INHABITING MECHANICAL SPACE

LOCATION: El Paso and Ciudad Juárez DESIGNER(s): Javier Breceda INSTITUTION: Texas Tech DESCRIPTION: The project maps levels of lead accumulation on-site, effectively highlighting intentional neglect and contamination caused by a blurred jurisdictional condition at the international border.

BINATIONAL SANITORIUM

LOCATION: El Paso and Ciudad Juárez DESIGNER(s): Lauren Carmona INSTITUTION: Texas Tech DESCRIPTION: Mitigating soil contamination within the jurisdictional bubble of the US-Mexico border.

MONARCH INFRASTRUCTURE

LOCATION: El Paso and Ciudad Juárez DESIGNER(s): Marilyn Reyes INSTITUTION: Texas Tech DESCRIPTION: Binational rest stop for migratory bodies. Seasonal migration patterns of monarch butterflies transcend the political border and highlight the futility of the fence.

INFRASTRUCTURAL SANITORIUM

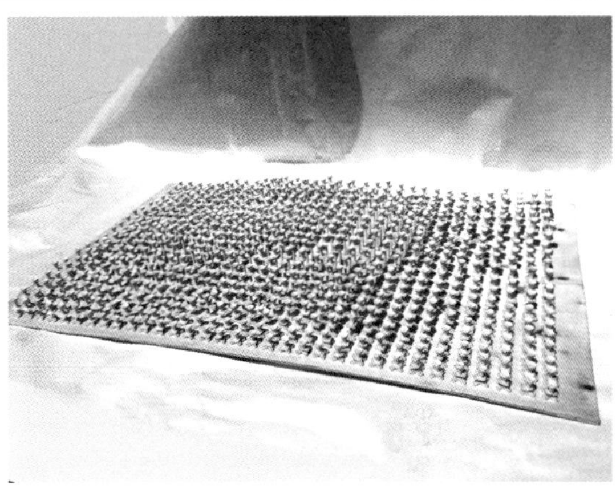

LOCATION: El Paso and Ciudad Juárez DESIGNER(s): Miguel Radilla INSTITUTION: Texas Tech DESCRIPTION: The project uses border infrastructure as a context for architectural space.

LIGHT OBJECT FIELD

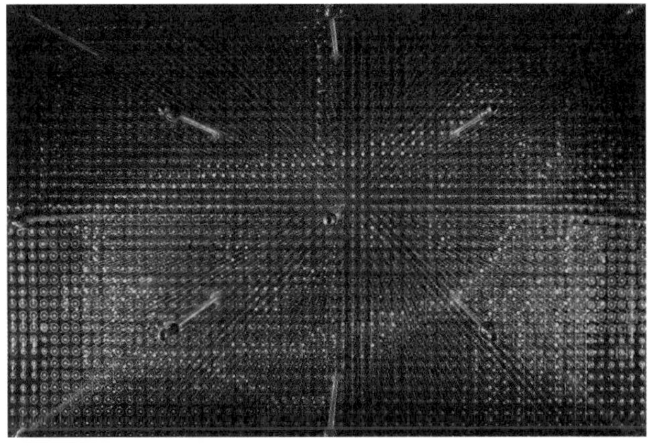

LOCATION: El Paso and Ciudad Juárez DESIGNER(s): Valente Leanos INSTITUTION: Texas Tech DESCRIPTION: Fighting light with light: a thick cloud of light to disorient border surveillance optics.

DESERT OPTICS

LOCATION: El Paso and Ciudad Juárez DESIGNER(s): Daniel Ramirez INSTITUTION: Texas Tech DESCRIPTION: Refracting the atmospheric optics of a desert crossing. The project elaborates a structural and spatial mechanism to manage elusive optical effects in a desert landscape.

MYCOLOGIC

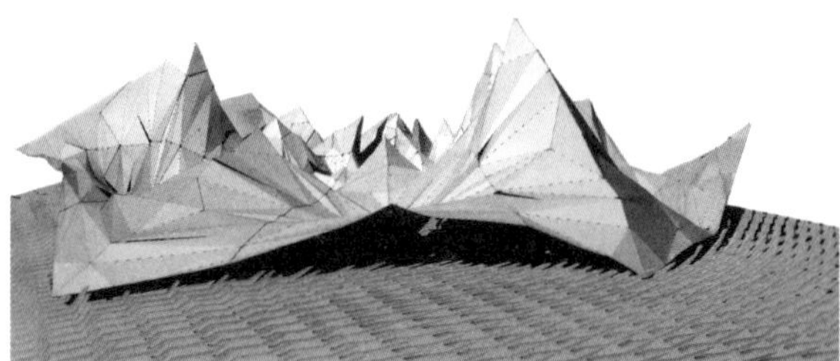

LOCATION: El Paso and Ciudad Juárez DESIGNER(s): Irving Cuellar INSTITUTION: Texas Tech DESCRIPTION: A center for the study of airborne biology in the borderland.

SMOG INSTITUTE

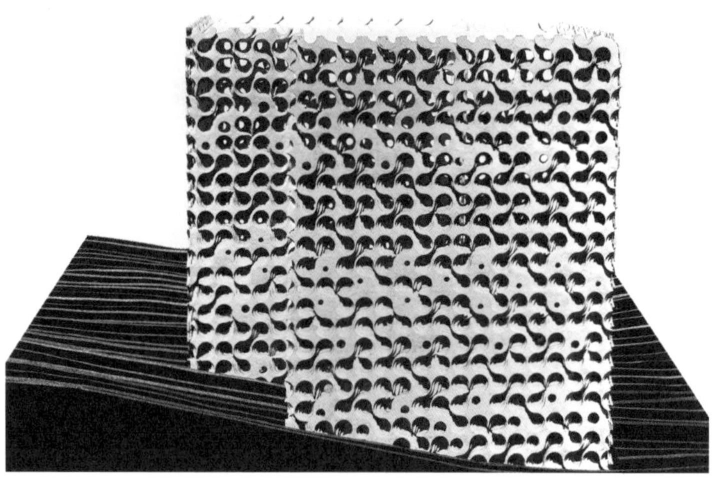

LOCATION: El Paso and Ciudad Juárez DESIGNER(s): Sabrina Schrader INSTITUTION: Texas Tech DESCRIPTION: A distillery for binational air pollution. The smog institute proposes a binational center to study and remediate cross-border airborne contaminants.

RADIOACTIVE ATMOSPHERE INSTITUTE

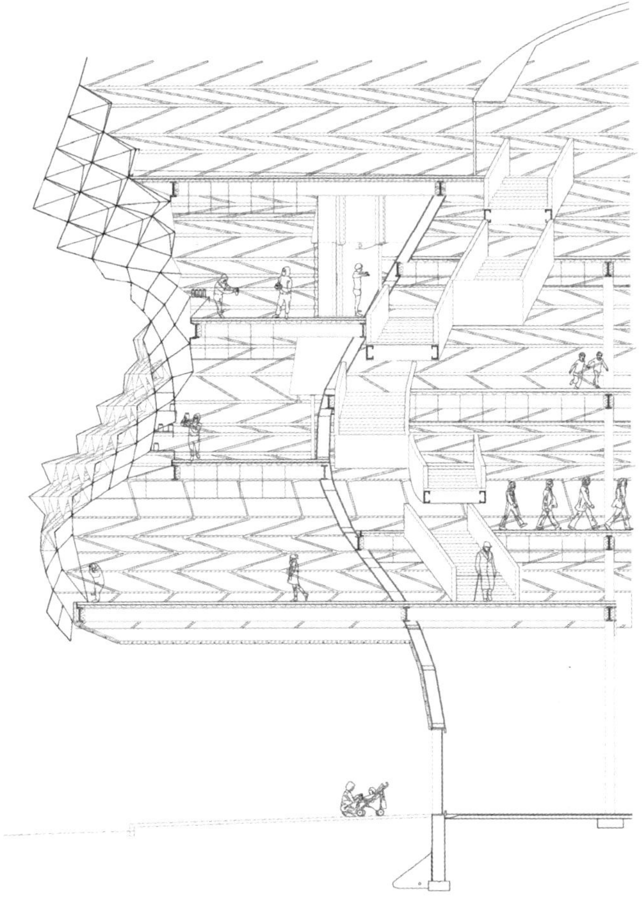

LOCATION: El Paso and Ciudad Juárez DESIGNER(s): Nathaniel Casana INSTITUTION: Texas Tech DESCRIPTION: Sensing aeolian isotopes in the radioactive borderlands. The building acts as a territorial filter and monitoring mechanism for windblown radioactive dust.

TURBULENCE INSTITUTE

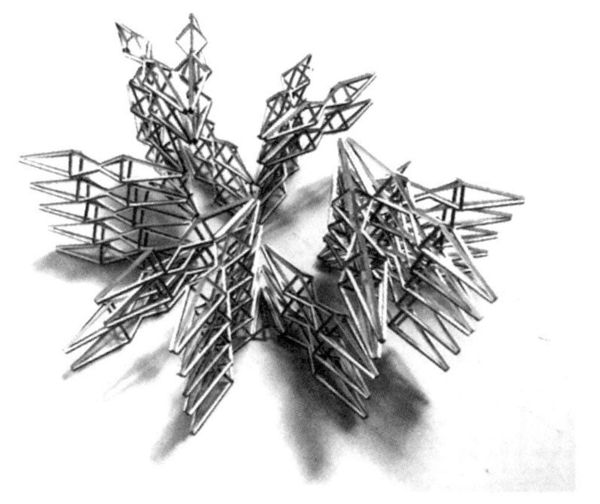

LOCATION: El Paso and Ciudad Juárez DESIGNER(s): Sergio Esquinca INSTITUTION: Texas Tech DESCRIPTION: An architectural machine to manage turbulent binational flows.

WATER A CITY

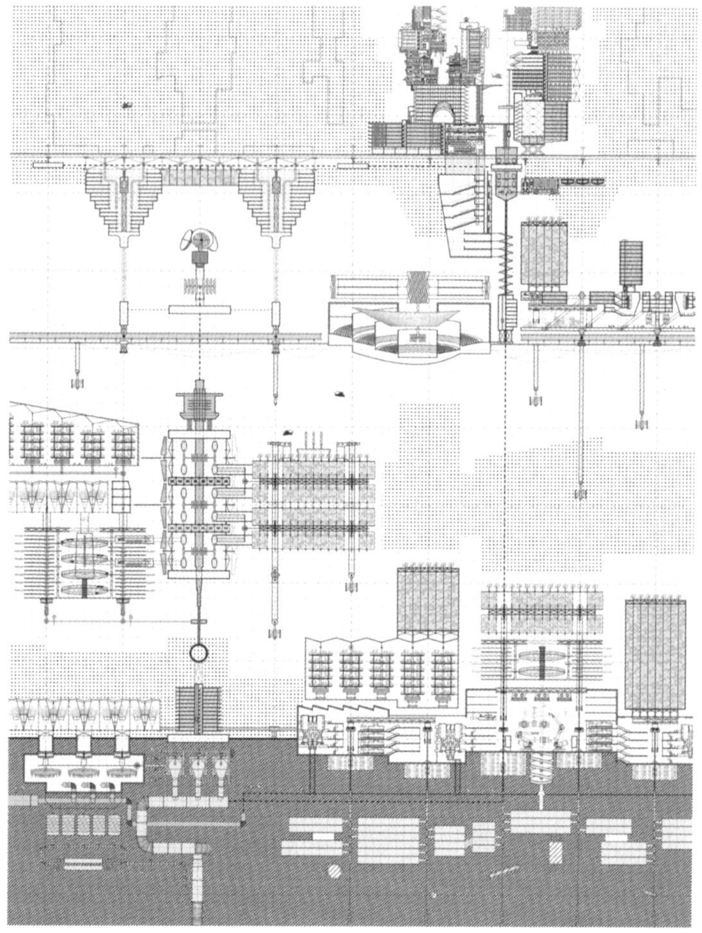

LOCATION: El Paso and Ciudad Juárez DESIGNER(s): Meng Ye, Han Zhang INSTITUTION: University of Michigan DESCRIPTION: A radical representation of capitalist-free zone of water.

TRAILHEAD INSTITUTE

LOCATION: El Paso and Ciudad Juárez DESIGNER(s): Kai Kang INSTITUTION: University of Michigan DESCRIPTION: The response to the river ecology, geology and spiritual significance of this transnational site.

NETWORK FOR THE REAPPROPRIATION OF HYDROLOGIC BY-PRODUCTS TRANSNATIONAL ECOLOGIES STUDIO

LOCATION: El Paso and Ciudad Juárez DESIGNER(s): Kevin Raley INSTITUTION: University of Michigan DESCRIPTION: Rather than affirming the conventional notions of product and waste, The Network studies the potential for all materials to play a positive role in the greater ecosystem.

MAKING WATER PUBLIC

LOCATION: El Paso and Ciudad Juárez DESIGNER(s): Ryan Wang INSTITUTION: University of Michigan DESCRIPTION: Making water public in the transborder area.

HAYDUKE CENTER FOR WATER INITIATIVES

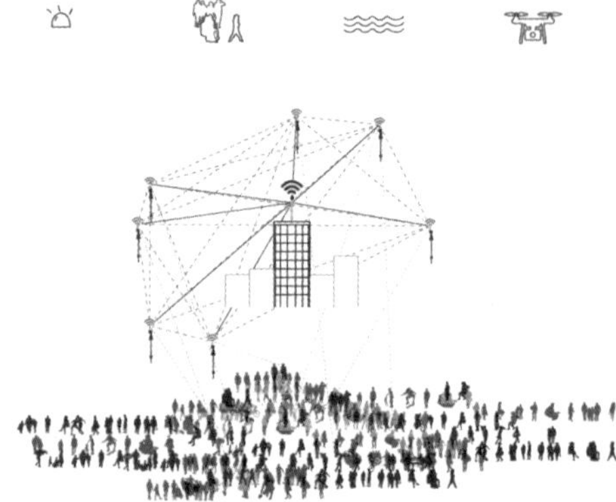

LOCATION: El Paso and Ciudad Juárez DESIGNER(s): Joshua Krell, Samuel P. Scardefield INSTITUTION: University of Michigan DESCRIPTION: The intent of this project is to simultaneously address urban gaps and infrastructural holes that have left many of the citizens in Ciudad Juárez behind.

TERCERA NACION PASO DEL NORTE INSTITUTE OF RIGHTS

LOCATION: El Paso and Ciudad Juárez DESIGNER(s): Shane P. Donnelly INSTITUTION: University of Michigan DESCRIPTION: An urban proposal for the US-Mexico border that produces a territorial manifestation of the "Third Nation", a concept proposed in Michael Deer's *Why Walls Won't Work*.

FRONTERIZA COMMUNITY CENTER

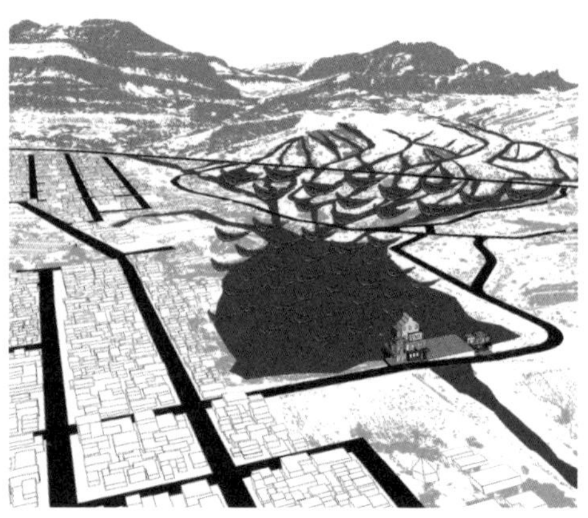

LOCATION: El Paso and Ciudad Juárez DESIGNER(s): Sneha Reddy INSTITUTION: University of Michigan DESCRIPTION: Flood mitigation and community gathering space.

WATER PARLIAMENT

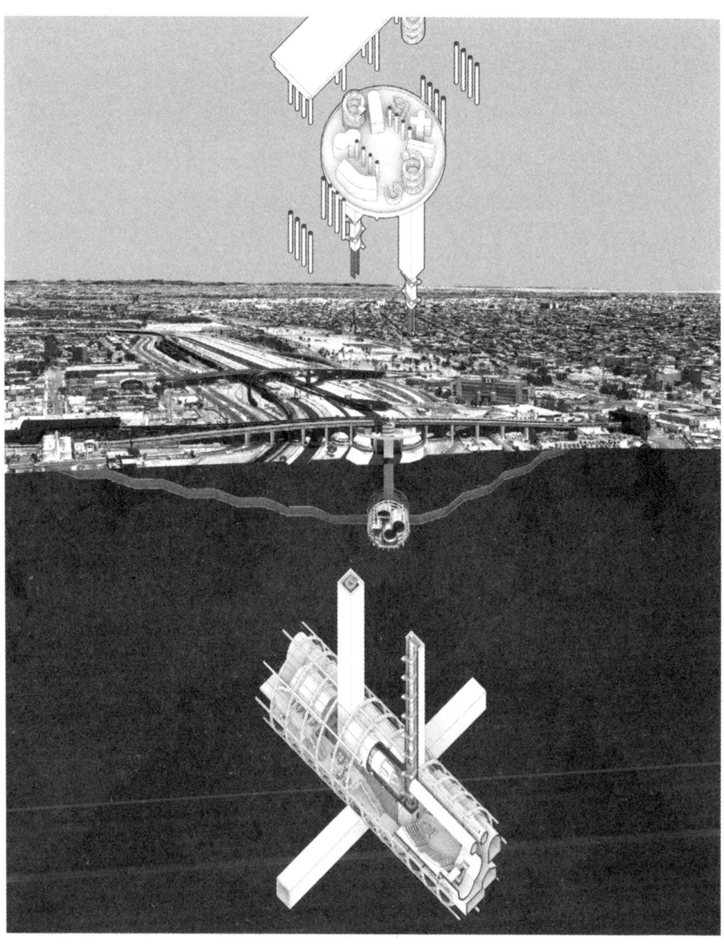

LOCATION: El Paso and Ciudad Juárez DESIGNER(s): Ziyuan Feng INSTITUTION: University of Michigan DESCRIPTION: A hybrid of typologies makes the border ambiguous again.

Farming, Agriculture and Migration

Undeterred by the desire for separate identities, trade agreements such as NAFTA reflect the intertwined destinies and influences of the US and Mexico. An exchange of food, labor, and commercial products and the interwoven production of goods have altered the economic landscape of the region. Produce exported from Mexico to the United States, quadrupled between 1990 and 2012, while the US was able to increase its exports of processed food to Mexico. This exchange connects not only the farming industries but also domestic life and kitchen tables of families throughout the US–Mexico Region, far from the border. Mexico has lost many farming jobs in the last two decades, encouraging additional labor migration to the United States. Sixty-eight percent of the three million migrant farm workers in the US are Mexican. The impact of antiimmigration efforts in the US exposes the importance of foreign labor in reviving small towns in the US. For example, of the approximately 6,000-person population of Ulysses, KS, half is Hispanic. The alternative to the diversifying town would be continued decline.

Karolina Czezek's studio Food Hub (University of Cincinnati) focused on industrial food production in the Ohio River valley, these international food centers supply food for the entire country. Ana Paula Ruiz Gallinda's studio Intersectional Landscapes (Cooper Union) focused on Mexican labor contributions to food production in Kansas. At Yale, the studio taught by Tatiana Bilbao proposed alternatives and projections to remap the "green prison system" to mitigate the exodus of farming labor to the United States and by retaining agricultural opportunities in Guanajuato and Hidalgo. The rural towns in central Mexico have been declining in population and the social systems that supported them. Physically tracing the movements of bodies and products demonstrates an interdependence that diffuses the border toward a new regionalism.

BIG BOX

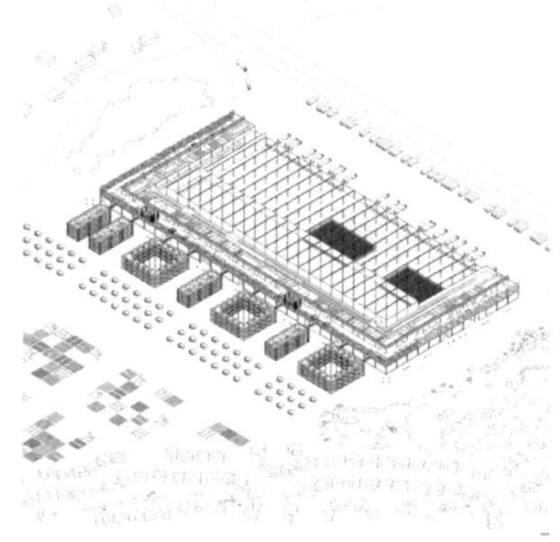

LOCATION: Columbus, Ohio DESIGNER(s): Amber Wasinski INSTITUTION: University of Cincinnati DESCRIPTION: Live-work big box community.

FOOD INCUBATOR

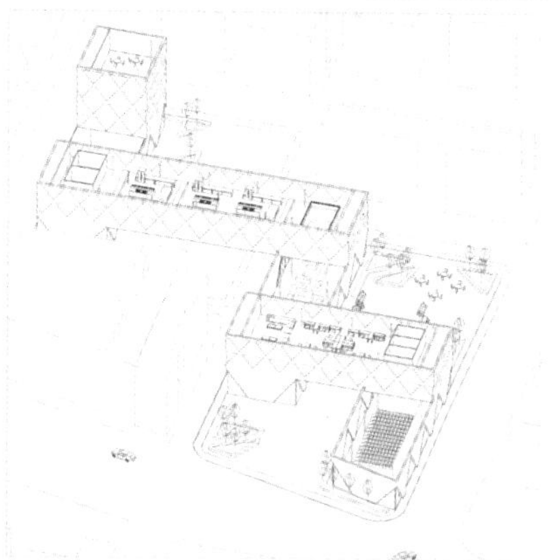

LOCATION: Columbus, Ohio DESIGNER(s): Courtney Kress INSTITUTION: University of Cincinnati DESCRIPTION: Food incubator and kitchen building.

GREENHOUSE COMMUNITY

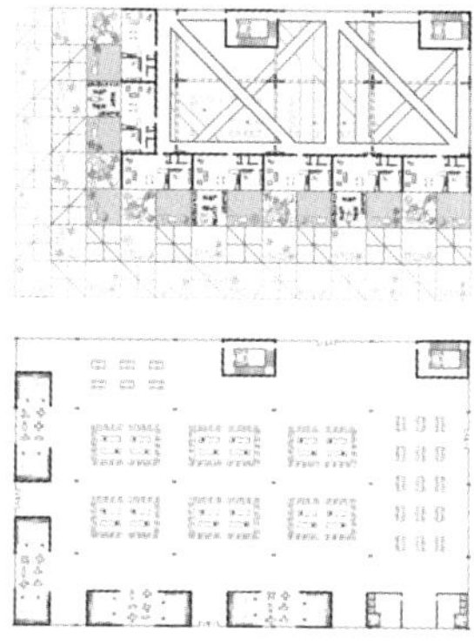

LOCATION: Columbus, Ohio DESIGNER(s): Dylan Stein INSTITUTION: University of Cincinnati DESCRIPTION: Housing project with urban farming.

FOOD EDUCATION HUB

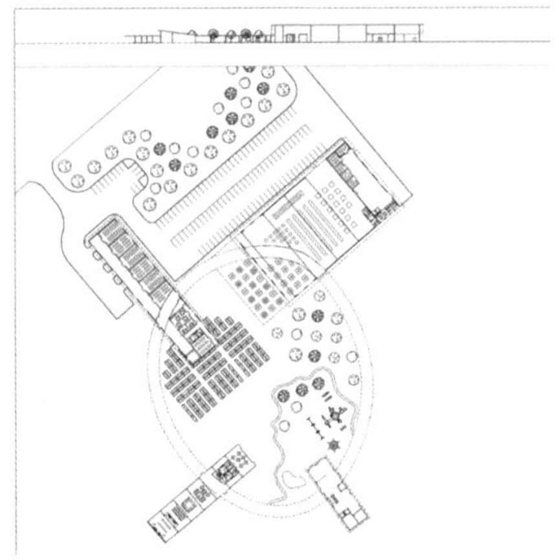

LOCATION: Columbus, Ohio DESIGNER(s): Emma Margerum-Leys INSTITUTION: University of Cincinnati DESCRIPTION: Food Hub in a local food desert.

AGRICULTURAL CITY

LOCATION: Columbus, Ohio DESIGNER(s): Justin Pang INSTITUTION: University of Cincinnati DESCRIPTION: Vision for an agricultural urbanism.

FRAMEWORK

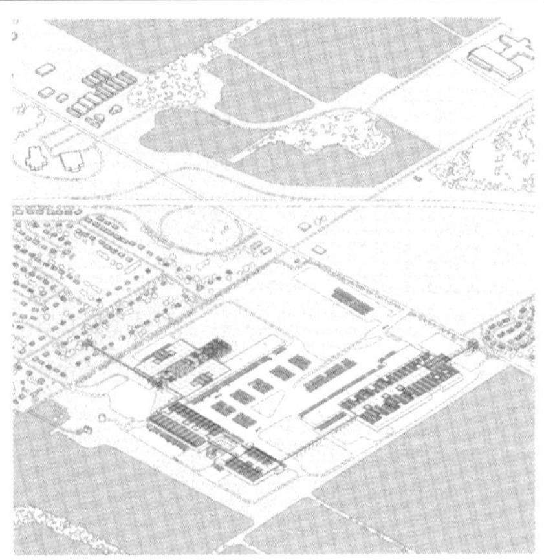

LOCATION: Columbus, Ohio DESIGNER(s): Nikki Weitz INSTITUTION: University of Cincinnati DESCRIPTION: Reuse of the logistical roofscape for food production.

FISH FARM

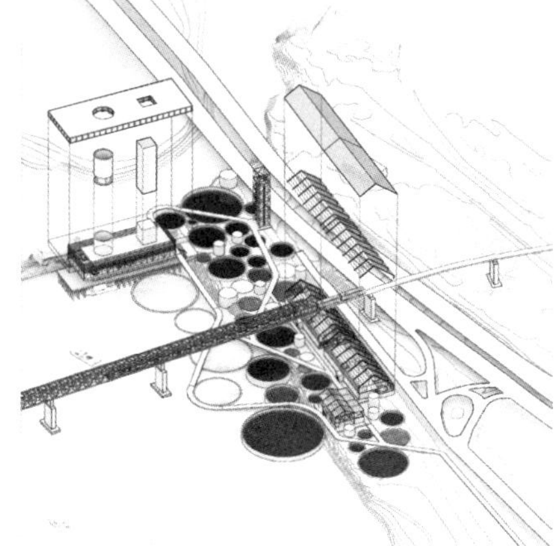

LOCATION: Columbus, Ohio DESIGNER(s): Ryan Detroit INSTITUTION: University of Cincinnati DESCRIPTION: Fish Farm park on the Ohio River.

FOOD MALL

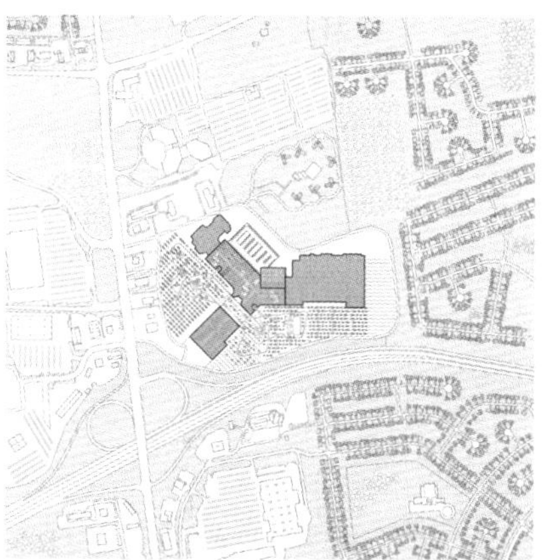

LOCATION: Columbus, Ohio DESIGNER(s): Unmesh Kelkar INSTITUTION: University of Cincinnati DESCRIPTION: Adaptive reuse of the abandoned shopping mall.

MUSHROOM FARM

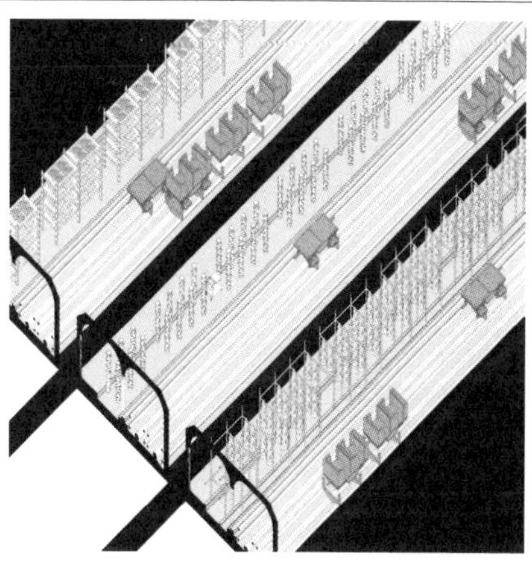

LOCATION: Columbus, Ohio DESIGNER(s): Varsha Iyengar INSTITUTION: University of Cincinnati DESCRIPTION: Abandoned subway reused for mushroom farming.

ELEVATED MOBILITY

LOCATION: Ulysses, Kansas DESIGNER(s): Cyrus Henry INSTITUTION: The Cooper Union DESCRIPTION: This project proposes transforming the aging infrastructure of the Great Plains to create a public transportation system accessible to immigrants.

ULYSSES LAND GROUP

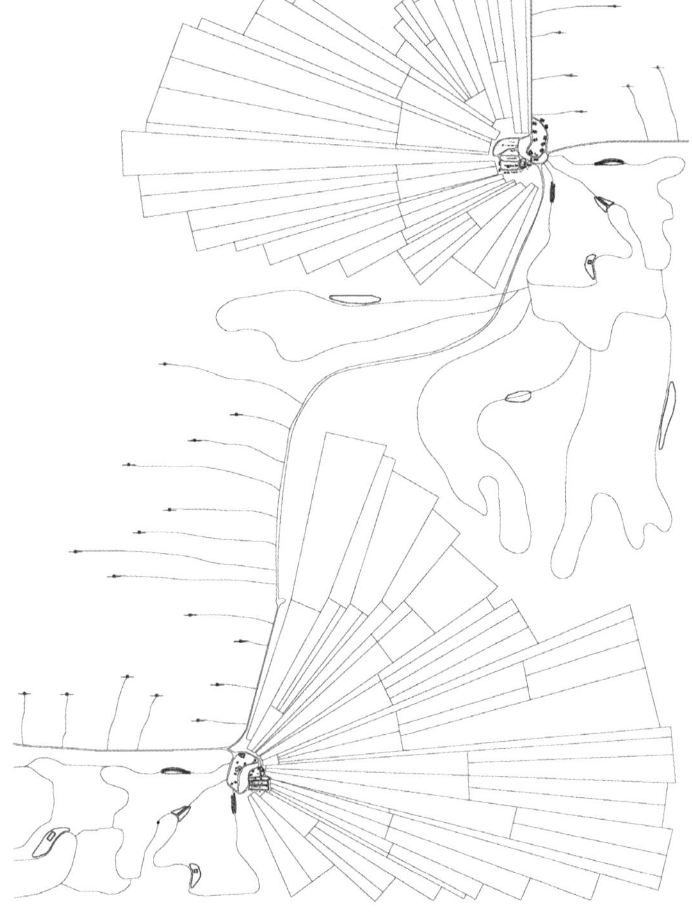

LOCATION: Ulysses, Kansas DESIGNER(s): Julia DiPietro INSTITUTION: The Cooper Union DESCRIPTION: At a moment of crisis, Kansas sheds its cartesian ethic of individualism and replaces it with a nodal ecosystem of land sharing.

INTO THE HORIZON

LOCATION: Ulysses, Kansas DESIGNER(s): Kari Opsal Maeland INSTITUTION: The Cooper Union DESCRIPTION: Reading history through the landscape.

ULYSSES' ODYSSEY

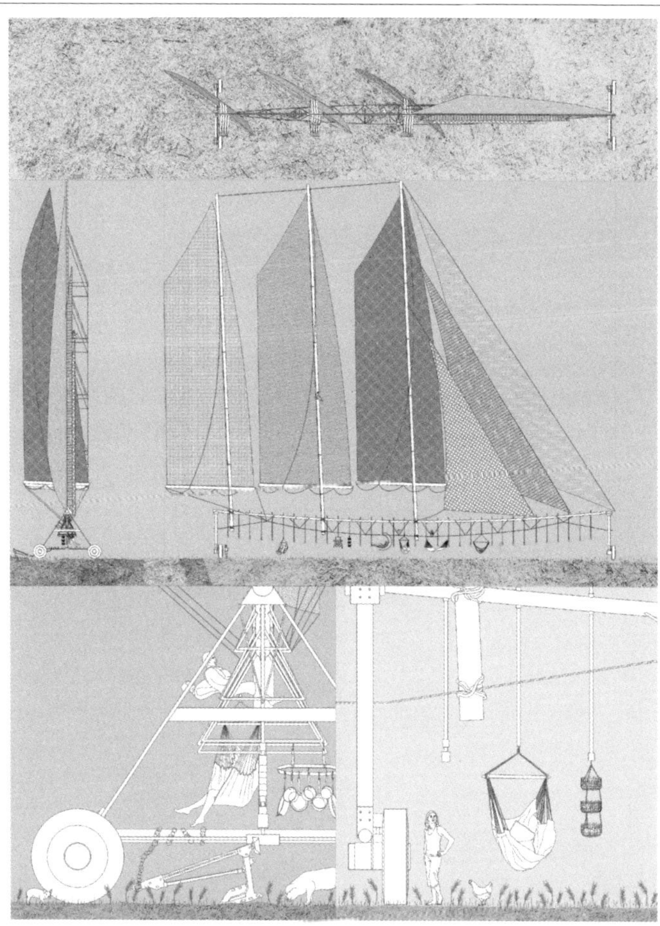

LOCATION: Ulysses, Kansas DESIGNER(s): Mireya Fabregas INSTITUTION: The Cooper Union DESCRIPTION: Propose a new type of nomadic living by tracing the history of the Great Plains through migration patterns to uncover the different identities that have inhabited the land.

UNIVERSAL SECRETARY

LOCATION: Ulysses, Kansas DESIGNER(s): Parker Limon INSTITUTION: The Cooper Union DESCRIPTION: An ATM that does more than take money out of your bank account.

THE FIFTH QUARTER

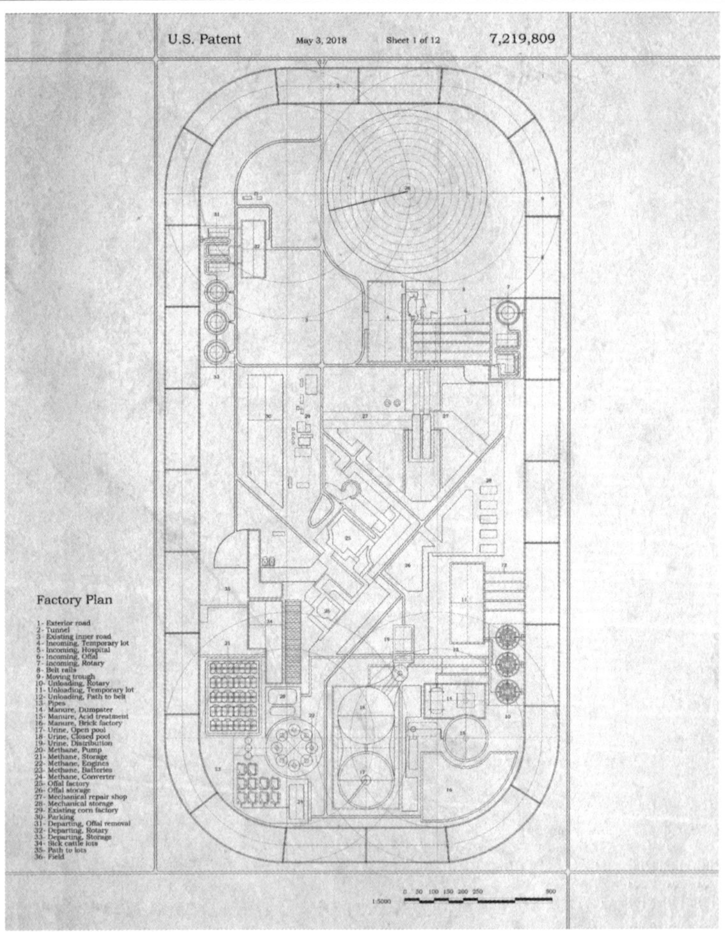

LOCATION: Ulysses, Kansas DESIGNER(s): Stav Eilam INSTITUTION: The Cooper Union DESCRIPTION: A portrait of capitalist society via Kansas's cattle industry.

FORT MOBILE

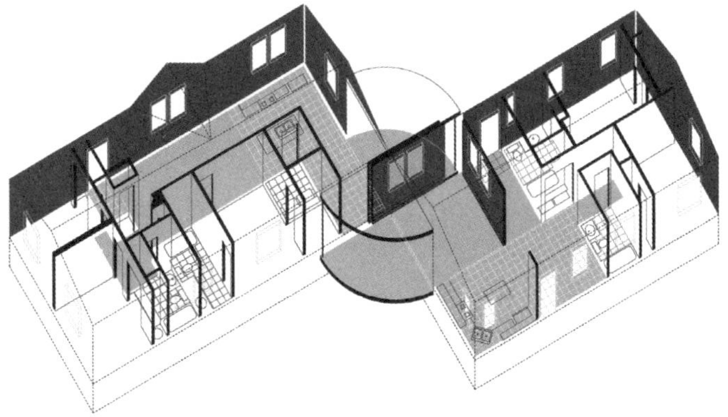

LOCATION: Ulysses, Kansas DESIGNER(s): Yuki Nakayama INSTITUTION: The Cooper Union DESCRIPTION: Mother as an activator for architecture and planning of a defensive community.

EL ALBERTO CHINAMPAS VILLAGE

LOCATION: Huanímaro, Guanajuato DESIGNER(s): Audrey Yifei Li INSTITUTION: Yale DESCRIPTION: This project seeks to regenerate communal agricultural practices through tackling the water issue in El Alberto, Ixmiquilpan.

SMALL WALLS

LOCATION: Huanímaro, Guanajuato DESIGNER(s): Amanda Iglesias INSTITUTION: Yale DESCRIPTION: Addressing the global agrarian crisis. This project presents a hortus (in)conclusus: a hybridized typology that merges the hacienda's perimeter grammar with the hortus conclusus, a walled garden typology rich with religious and allegorical iconography.

GARDEN OF REDEMPTION

LOCATION: Zimápan, Hidalgo DESIGNER(s): Hyeree Kwak INSTITUTION: Yale DESCRIPTION: Beauty and hope in a place of waste and neglect.

SORGO COLECTIVO

LOCATION: Pénjamo, Guanajuato DESIGNER(s): J. Javier Perez INSTITUTION: Yale DESCRIPTION: A worker's collective in the center of Pénjamo processing sorghum, used for brooms, furniture and woven goods, to provide new opportunities for the community.

SAN FRANCISCO ACADEMIC VILLAGE

LOCATION: Zimápan, Hidalgo DESIGNER(s): Karen Delgado INSTITUTION: Yale DESCRIPTION: Reshaping education and construction in remote villages.

INVERTED FACTORIES

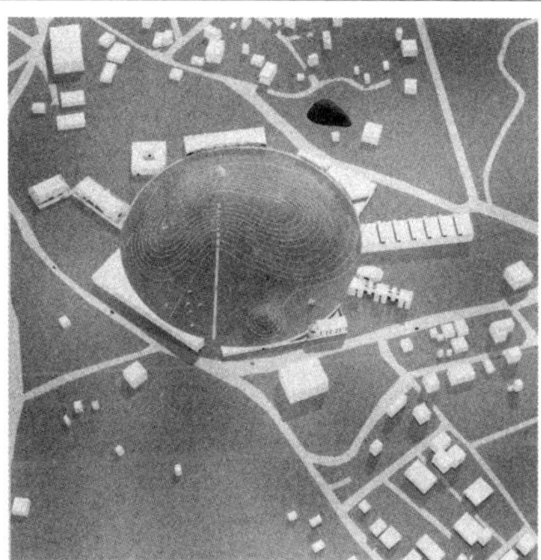

LOCATION: Zimápan, Hidalgo DESIGNER(s): Kevin Huang INSTITUTION: Yale DESCRIPTION: To save themselves from arsenic pollution, the people of Zimápan start a construction cooperative that is built around a park.

HUANIMARO KILNS

LOCATION: Huanímaro, Guanajuato DESIGNER(s): Laura Quan INSTITUTION: Yale DESCRIPTION: This project redirects the existing funding streams toward the construction of a brick factory, which would allow for the engagement of the city while continuing to provide the sustainable stream of construction materials.

THE PULQUE RITUAL

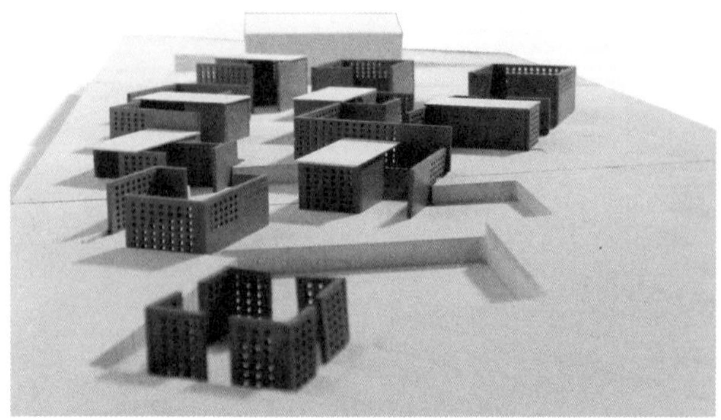

LOCATION: La Heredad, Hidalgo DESIGNER(s): Maria Isabel Balda INSTITUTION: Yale DESCRIPTION: Small rural towns like La Heredad still largely depend on agriculture for their economic output. The proposal introduces a maguey and pulque production complex that reintroduces a communal model of agricultural production to the community.

LOST TOWNS OF LA PRESA SOLIS

LOCATION: Acámbaro, Guanajuato DESIGNER(s): Matthew Dean Shaffer INSTITUTION: Yale DESCRIPTION: A landscape where the lost towns of the valleys east of Acámbaro have their presence marked again. The reclamation of ruins offers opportunities for new places of memory and reestablish relationships to the water beyond.

“DOMESTIC CRITIQUE”

LOCATION: Acámbaro, Guanajuato DESIGNER(s): Mariana Riobom INSTITUTION: Yale DESCRIPTION: The project places domestic labor, kitchens, laundries and small child and elder care centers into strategic public spaces across Acámbaro, socializing and professionalizing it, being performed by both men and women.

Growth and Cities

The role of urbanization should not be underemphasized in this project. The economic, cultural and political growth of cities is leading toward a simultaneous densification of cities and emptying-out of agricultural land. Agricultural land is no longer partially self-sustaining, but a machine to satisfy the demands of cities. For economic opportunities, many migrants move from rural towns to cities, both across the border as well as within Mexico. The demand for urban housing in cities like Monterrey and Austin are producing a new set of demands for cities, new versions of suburbia and dramatic increases in housing costs. The money gained from urban professions is also flowing back to rural towns in the form of remittances. Mexican immigrants in the US are known to form cooperative groups that send money back to their shared hometown to build critical infrastructure for their families and children.

Tatiana Bilbao's studio at GSAPP drew on the Sears Catalog houses of the 1950s US and the recent growth in remittance houses to propose aesthetic recalibrations, or new styles of houses that move beyond traditional US aesthetics to include vernacular architecture. The projects advanced the language of building manuals. While some of the networks involve the movement of money, labor or food, others involve cities on both sides of the border that face similar challenges and opportunities. Juan Miró's studio highlights one of these scenarios by analyzing, comparing and proposing future housing, tech and economic developments in Austin, Texas, and Monterrey, Nuevo León. Jorge Salinas's studio at Universidad de Monterrey offers an alternative perspective on Monterrey by focusing on mixed-use housing proposals. The Resilient City: Proposals for the Future of Mexico City taught by Robert Hutchinson and Jeff Hou at the University of Washington took on current crises in Mexico City to propose ambitious resolutions for a near future, like overscaled mechanized water infrastructure.

MODULAR URBAN INFILL

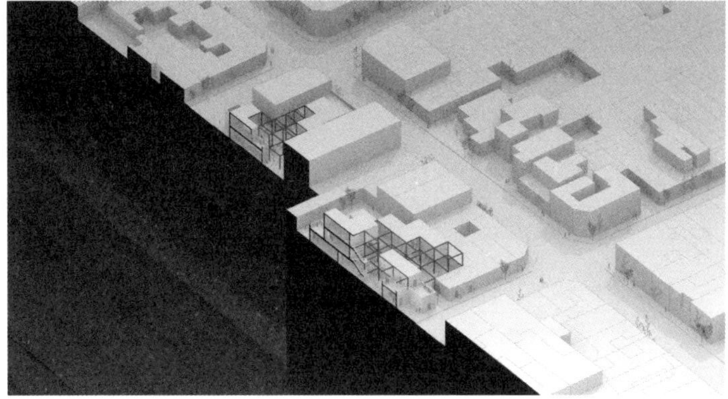

LOCATION: Monterrey, Nuevo León DESIGNER(s): Annie Liu INSTITUTION: UT Austin DESCRIPTION: In order to restore population levels in one of the oldest residential neighborhoods of Monterrey, this urban infill strategy targets underutilized properties and auto-related programs with a modular massing strategy that stretches the idea of the threshold into a new connective space that maintains the existing scale of the block.

COMMUNITY SUPERBLOCK

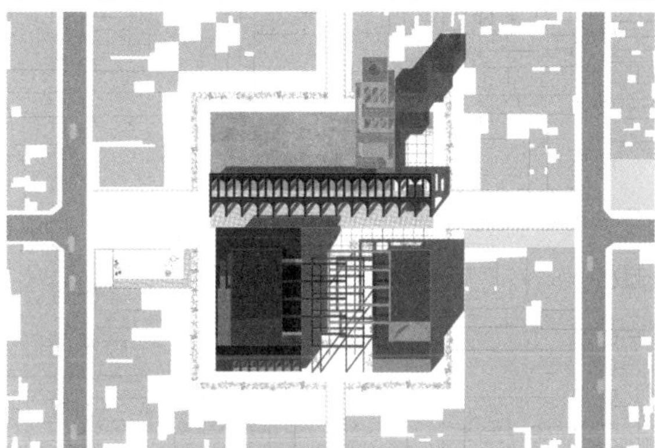

LOCATION: Monterrey, Nuevo León DESIGNER(s): Brooke Burnside, Savannah Simenhoff INSTITUTION: UT Austin DESCRIPTION: Understanding this proposal as a prototype for various scales of neighborhoods in Monterrey, the superblock demonstrates great potential to give back to the community directly surrounding it through the use of strategic programming and large public spaces.

LA ORILLA—RIVERFRONT PROPOSAL, MONTERREY

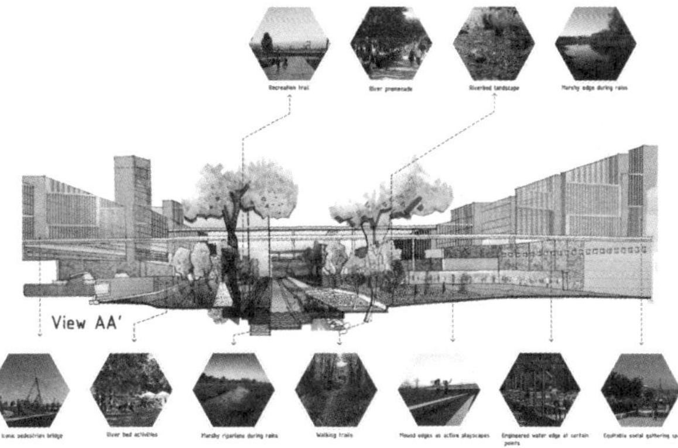

LOCATION: Monterrey, Nuevo León DESIGNER(s): Disha Sahu, Priya Patel INSTITUTION: UT Austin DESCRIPTION: Our proposal of Santa Catarina Riverfront development aims to bring the north and the south banks of the city together through the creation of an active, green and accessible riverfront and riverbed design. The proposal integrates stormwater management, flood mitigation and space for active recreation for the city of Monterrey.

PASEO DE LAS GALERIAS

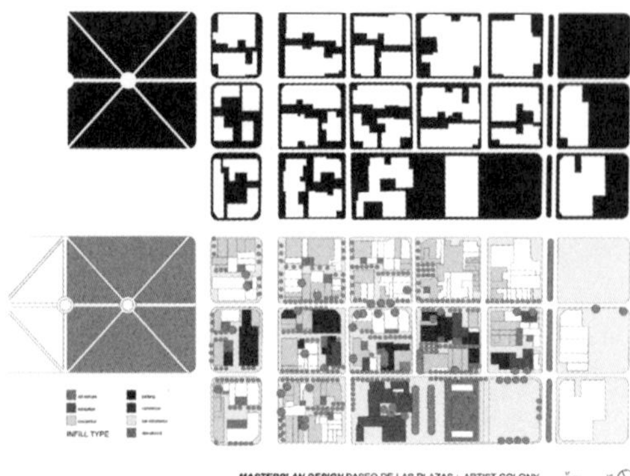

LOCATION: Monterrey, Nuevo León DESIGNER(s): Hannah Ahlblad INSTITUTION: UT Austin DESCRIPTION: Paseo de las Galerias proposes utilizing the building footprints of abandoned lots to open the block for a dynamic promenade, dense studio housing and a series of small garden "rooms" filled with outdoor artist installation, and pop-up events that weave together Monterrey's disjointed zone of museums, schools and theaters.

URBAN ENCLAVE: SERIES 1

LOCATION: Monterrey, Nuevo León DESIGNER(s): Shani Saul, Kat Hallisey INSTITUTION: UT Austin DESCRIPTION: The proposal is one implementation of a new method of development which can come to infuse abandoned and underutilized land on and around the site with mixed-use programming while additionally challenging the tabul.

THE BIKE COMMUNE

LOCATION: Monterrey, Nuevo León DESIGNER(s): Kim Choy, Sydney Moore INSTITUTION: UT Austin DESCRIPTION: The bike commune proposes a new mode of dwelling and moving within Monterrey by reconciling the mobility infrastructure as both a system for soft mobility and a spatial object.

LA CENTRO DE LUTO Y REMEMBRANZA

LOCATION: Monterrey, Nuevo León DESIGNER(s): Mabel S.W. Loh INSTITUTION: UT Austin DESCRIPTION: A site for mourning, remembrance and celebration unique to the culture of Mexico.

TERRAZAS LA ORILLA

LOCATION: Monterrey, Nuevo León DESIGNER(s): Sara Ramirez, Philip Richardson INSTITUTION: UT Austin DESCRIPTION: Terrazas La Orilla is the first development of riverfront architecture in Monterrey, providing housing, public amenities and substantial parking in an iconic arrangement of objects engaging the new linear park.

CAMPO CENTRAL DE LA UNIVERSIDAD METROPOLITANA DE MONTERREY

LOCATION: Monterrey, Nuevo León DESIGNER(s): Valentina Rodriguez INSTITUTION: UT Austin DESCRIPTION: El Campo Central de la Universidad Metropolitana de Monterrey reimagines three existing large city blocks, comprised of underutilized lots and abandoned buildings, into an urban opportunity to connect and develop civic buildings in Downtown Monterrey through the creation of a central core campus that guides visitors across the Macroplaza toward the new Plaza Benito Juárez.

AKTAAN

LOCATION: Monterrey, Nuevo León DESIGNER(s): Debanhi Ramos, Mariana Jauregui Perez INSTITUTION: University of Monterrey DESCRIPTION: The AKTAAN cultural center located in front of Purisima Plaza in downtown Monterrey. The surrounding urban space is currently neglected and abandoned, this proposal was designed as a possible response to revert this condition and to cultural diversity in society.

PROYECTO TS-J

LOCATION: Monterrey, Nuevo León DESIGNER(s): Francisco Javier Serrano Alanis, Miguel Angel Torres Monarrez INSTITUTION: University of Monterrey DESCRIPTION: Reinterpretation of urban life through multifamily development.

TORRE HIDALGO

LOCATION: Monterrey, Nuevo León DESIGNER(s): Patricia Ayala, Sara Mendez INSTITUTION: University of Monterrey DESCRIPTION: A place for everyone—replaces Departments Zambrano, which has been completely abandoned and neglected for many years.

MARKET AND CULINARY CENTER

LOCATION: Monterrey, Nuevo León DESIGNER(s): Alfredo Davila, Priscila Ramirez, Grecia Manzo INSTITUTION: University of Monterrey DESCRIPTION: With the aim of revitalizing and regenerating the metropolitan center of Monterrey, our project for a downtown market building seeks to have a positive impact not only on the urban context, but on the local society in general.

NEW STRUCTURES FOR LIVING

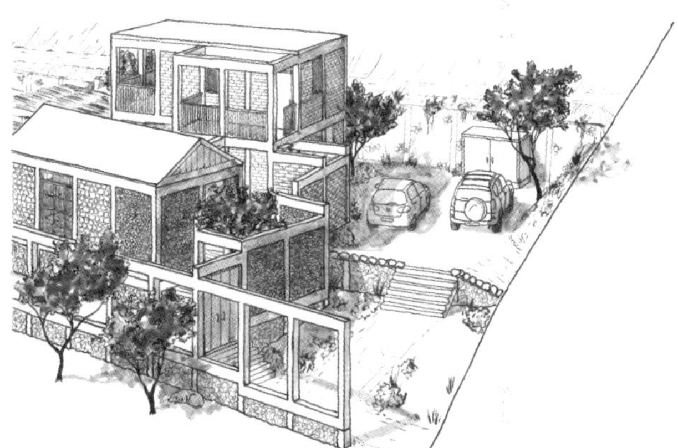

LOCATION: Ixpantepec Nieves DESIGNER(s): Colin Matthews INSTITUTION: Columbia GSAPP DESCRIPTION: A family of homes for Ixpantepec Nieves, Oaxaca.

THE CASE OF JOSE

LOCATION: Mineral de Pozos DESIGNER(s): Minjae Kim INSTITUTION: Columbia GSAPP DESCRIPTION: Returning homo; brick by brick. A typological combination of a colonial courtyard and a Texas shed house to take advantage of the emerging tourist economy in Mineral de Pozos.

OAXACA INFONAVIT, REMODELED

LOCATION: Oaxaca DESIGNER(s): Masha Konopleva INSTITUTION: Columbia GSAPP DESCRIPTION: From Oaxaca to Poughkeepsie and back to Oaxaca: a remittance home for the retiring Mexican-American. Seeing to create communal space for an extended family in rural Oaxaca while affording residents the privacy and luxury of their own, unique homes.

THE WINDOWED HUT

LOCATION: Oxkutzcab DESIGNER(s): Mouna Lawrence INSTITUTION: Columbia GSAPP DESCRIPTION: After living and working in San Francisco for twenty years, two brothers from the Yucatán peninsula look to the hybridization of the American bay window and traditional Mayan in designing and constructing their family home and a school.

THE MANUAL OF EARTH BLOCK ARCHITECTURE

LOCATION:None DESIGNER(s):Tonia Sing Chi INSTITUTION:Columbia GSAPP DESCRIPTION:Compressed earth block is proposed as a construction process that activates a set of possibilities, allowing for individual expression and autonomy.

BLOCKS MANUAL

LOCATION:Puebla DESIGNER(s):Ronald Yeung INSTITUTION:Columbia GSAPP DESCRIPTION:The remittance style of mass customization. A structural and typological system that allows people to personalize their homes and studios—inspired by the American culture of mass customization.

THE BLUE RING:CLAIMING WATER SANCTUARY

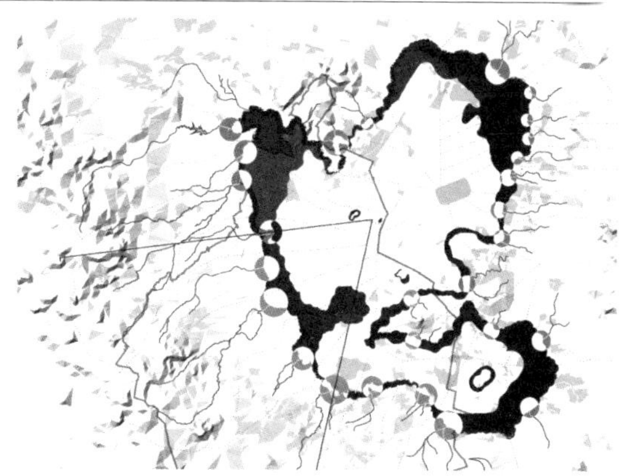

LOCATION:Mexico City DESIGNER(s):Kelsey Pierson, Roxanne Glick, Yang Su INSTITUTION:University of Washington DESCRIPTION:Building a Culture of Resilience. Due to high demand, Mexico City's main source of potable water is being depleted faster than it can be replenished. This project aims to empower these impoverished people as guardians of this valuable land that serves the whole city.

ARCHITECTURE ON REVOLUTION

LOCATION: Mexico City DESIGNER(s): Veronica Leanos, Gabrielle Lewis, John Rodezno INSTITUTION: University of Washington
DESCRIPTION: A revolution has occurred, attempting to call attention to the growing disparity of neighborhoods such as Santa Fe.

POROCITY

LOCATION: Mexico City DESIGNER(s): Melissa Marquez, Ilse Torres, Lauren Wabiszewski INSTITUTION: University of Washington
DESCRIPTION: Integrated elements of water, green space and urban elements that create a self-sustainable development for Valle de Chalco, ultimately leading to a large-scale return of Lake Texcoco.

CENTROS

LOCATION: Mexico City DESIGNER(s): Amy Broska, Melinda Groenewegen, Xu Fengyi INSTITUTION: University of Washington DESCRIPTION: This project proposes a city-wide hub system that supports flexible public services, activities and shelter for daily, special events and disaster use.

CENTRAL MIXED-USE COMMUNITY

LOCATION: Mexico City DESIGNER(s): Carlos Ortega Quintanar INSTITUTION: Universidad Iberoamericana DESCRIPTION: Central Mixed-Use Building responding to the limited free space in the city.

CRAFTSMEN COMMUNITY

LOCATION: Mexico City DESIGNER(s): Felipe Lelo de Larrea INSTITUTION: Universidad Iberoamericana DESCRIPTION: A new vertical community for artists and craftsmen.

MATERIA TOWER

LOCATION: Mexico City DESIGNER(s): Carolina Carselle Castello INSTITUTION: Universidad Iberoamericana DESCRIPTION: Materia Tower is conceived as an interdisciplinary complex dedicated to the conservation and appreciation of Mexican design.

This project has left us all indebted to the people who have helped. There has been an incredible amount of effort and love poured into this project to reimagine the region between the US and Mexico.

First of all, we'd like to thank Deborah Berke, who spurred the first steps in the project and invited us to expand with an exhibition at Yale and this book.

Thank you to Lars Müller who has always been a supporter of our work and these kinds of projects that pull together far-flung ideas into beautiful books.

Iwan Baan resides as the central artist — who captured the region with the perfect blend of naivety, compassion, precision and appreciation. We want to thank him for all the work and travel he did with haste.

We want to thank Ayesha S. Ghosh, the assistant editor and assistant curator on the project, who has carried this project on behalf of the Tatiana Bilbao Estudio with intelligence, tenacity and care. Without her this project would have not been possible. I want to also thank Alba Cortés, Sebastián Vizcaíno, Gabriela Álvarez and Juan Pablo Ponce de Leon, who worked diligently on this project from within the office as well. We extend our gratitude to Catia Bilbao and Juan Pablo Benlliure, the partners in Tatiana Bilbao Estudio who ensure we have the support and resources to pursue radical projects.

Amale Andraos from Columbia GSAPP was also a great supporter of the initiative and invited a bold group of masters students to work on the project with us.

Thank you to Valeria Luiselli and her niece Ana Puente Flores for being incredible inspiring figures in their work, commitment to the truths of this project and their advocacy for the regional imagination. Thank you especially to Valeria for coming to visit our studio at Columbia and inspiring a voice for the project.

Thank you to Sarah Lynn Lopez, whose work on remittance houses was both an inspiration for our work and an invaluable insight into the phenomenon.

Thank you to all of our exhibition hosts. Andrew Brenner and Alison Walsh from Yale worked incredibly hard to stage the first exhibition and without their efforts, much of the beauty of the project would be lost. Thanks to Laura Coombs, who designed the graphics for the first exhibition and gave our project an alphabet to speak with. Thank you to Hans-Jürgen Commerell and Mathias Schnell from AEDES Architekturforum in Berlin for staging the exhibition in the city where we learned how to topple walls. Thank you Ersela Kripa and Stephen Mueller for bringing the show to El Paso, where our work finally returned to the border. Thank you to Texas Tech El Paso and the El Paso Museum of Art for supporting the project.

There are two wonderful editors to thank — Walter Ancarrow who edited the majority of this book and time after time impressed authors with his cunning edits. Thank you to Mary Rose MacDonald who transcribed the interviews quickly and crafted and converted language into bright statements.

Thanks to Luke Bulman for designing the book; his work gives order, clarity and intention to the project.

Thank you to our friends who chimed in, asked what we were working on and offered opinions, advice and patience when necessary: Lucy Weisner, Matthew Kennedy, Ben Ganz, Enzo Valerio, Michael Abel, Isabelle Kirkham-Lewitt and Zachary White.

Thank you to all the professors who took a bold step of joining the initiative from the beginning and engaging their students and universities in the project: Raveevarn Choksombatchai, Karolina Czeczek, Ana Paula Ruiz Galindo, Mecky Reuss, Derek Dellekamp, Rozana Montiel, Kathy Velikov, Ersela Kripa, Stephen Mueller, Jorge Eduardo Galván Salinas, Juan Pablo Serrano Orozco, Salvador Rivas Trujillo, Juan Miró, David Bruton Jr., Robert Hutchison, Jeff Hou and Andrei Harwell.

To all of the students who participated, thank you all deeply for being the energy, the enthusiasm and the engine of this project. Your work has inspired so many new ideas.

From University of California Berkeley: Drishya Chhetri, Siamak Saadati, Felix Yiu, Parama Suteja, Kevin Aviles, Aboubacar Komara, Matt Giles, Hao Wang, Paola, Noemi Gutierrez, Sangjin Joung, Tiange Wang, Margaret Zhou and Yunbo Yan.

Within the University of Cincinnati: Amber Wasinski, Colin Martin, Courtney Kress, Dylan Stein, Emma Margerum-Leys, Justin Pang, Nikki Weitz, Ryan Detroit, Unmesh Kelkar and Varsha Iyengar.

Inside The Cooper Union: Asbjørn Eriknauer, Cyrus Henry, Julia DiPietro, Kari, Opsal Maeland, Mireya Fábregas, Parker Limón, Stav Eilam and Yuki Nakayama.

At Cornell University: Christina Zau, Isabella Hübsch, Ellen Park, Yue Ma, Hallie Black, Hyojin Lee, Kaylin Park, Yue Ma, Ellen Park and Kaylin Park.

Above Avery Library at Columbia University, GSAPP: Colin Matthews, Masha Konopleva, Minjae Kim, Mouna Lawrence, Ronald Yeung and Tonia Sing Chi.

On the campus of the University of Michigan: Meng Ye, Han Zhang, Kai Kang, Kevin Raley, Ryan Wang, Joshua Krell, Samuel P. Scardefield, Shane P. Donnelly, Sneha Reddy and Ziyuan Feng.

In the Amtrak station at Texas Tech El Paso: Alexandra Cortez, Daniel Rios,

Javier Breceda, Jonathan Fierro, Lauren Carmona, Marilyn Reyes, Miguel Radilla and Valente Leanos. Daniel Ramirez, Irving Cuellar, Nathaniel Casana, Sabrina Schrader and Sergio Esquinca.

En La Universidad de Monterrey: Debanhi Ramos, Mariana Jauregui Perez, Mauricio Oliva, Rossana Garza, Francisco Javier Serrano Alanís, Miguel Ángel Torres Monárrez, Patricia Ayala, Sara Méndez, Alfredo Davila, Priscila Ramiro and Grecia Manzo.

Cerca de Mexico City en la Universidad Iberoamericana: Carlos Ortega Quintanar, Carolina Carselle Castello, Felipe Lelo de Larrea and Valeria Lopez Castelazo.

Near the capitol at the University of Texas at Austin: Annie Liu, Brooke Burnside, Savannah Simenhoff, Disha Sahu, Priya Patel, Hannah Ahlblad, Shani Saul, Kat Hallisey, Kim Choy, Sydney Moore, Mabel S. W. Loh, Sara Ramirez, Philip Richardson and Valentina Rodriguez.

On the Canadian Border at the University of Washington: Veronica Leanos, Gabrielle Lewis, John Rodezno, Kelsey Pierson, Roxanne Glick, Yang Su, Melissa Marquez, Ilse Torres, Lauren Wabiszewski, Yuansi Cai, Annalisa Castelli, Richard Hua, Laura Durgerian, Mackinley Erickson, Sharon Fung, Amy Broska, Melinda Groenewegen and Xu Fengyi.

In the stacked hallways of Yale: Amanda Iglesias, Audrey Yifei Li, Hyeree Kwak, J. Javier Perez, Jeongyoon Isabelle Song, Karen Delgado, Kevin Huang, Laura Quan, Maria Isabel Balda, Mariana Riobom and Matthew Dean Shaffer.

Thank you everyone.

— Tatiana, Nile and Ayesha

Two Sides of the Border: Reimagining the Region

In collaboration with the Yale School of Architecture

The book is conceived by Tatiana Bilbao Estudio.

Editors: Tatiana Bilbao, Nile Greenberg and Ayesha S. Ghosh

Translations: Fionn Petch (Spanish–English)
Copyediting: Walter Ancarrow
Proofreading: Keonaona Peterson

Design: Office of Luke Bulman
Printing and binding: Regal Printing, Hong Kong
Paper: Finnish Book 80, South Korea Matte 140
Type: Untitled Sans and MS Mincho

Additional support has been generously provided by Elise Jaffe + Jeffrey Brown and The Yale School of Architecture Dean's Discretionary Fund

Lars Müller Publishers is supported by the Swiss Federal Office of Culture with a structural contribution for the years 2016–2020.

Lars Müller Publishers
Zürich, Switzerland
www.lars-mueller-publishers.com

ISBN 978-3-03778-608-6

Distributed in North America by ARTBOOK | D.A.P.
www.artbook.com

Printed in China

What Remains

Living in the border has made us witnesses to the devastation of the individual that occurs today right in front of our eyes. Unfortunately, this phenomenon replicates along many borders. Immigrants are forced to escape the horror they live in their countries, having no other choice than to take this traumatic journey. People are stripped from their land, home, economy, identity, language, and most of them are left with no personal belongings to survive the basic human needs. Confronted with a population who feels threatened by them, immigrants stand alone and deprived from their human rights.

The contemporary still lifes captured in this series speak of an ephemeral world that forces us to rediscover the journey of the migrant, a hero of our time trapped between two increasingly cruel worlds. The intention is to approach the intimacy of stories of migrants and we start this series with families from El Salvador, Guatemala and Nicaragua. Men, women and children who have experienced in their own flesh the hostility of a trip that apparently has no final destination. Their few possessions, which are often the only thing that connects them to the warmth of their origin, function as survival kits that keep them alive in threatening moments.

These photographs were taken in July and August 2019 on the border of Ciudad Juárez and El Paso, Texas. It is necessary to put a spotlight to the dignity and resistance of these travelers, it is urgent that our society learns how to see, it is necessary to deactivate the discourses of hatred and racism. Very few dare to understand a new way of appreciating this type of resilience, resilience to survive.

— Monica Lozano and Samuel Rodriguez

Coca-Cola

MAKE
YOUR
Magic

Can We Play?

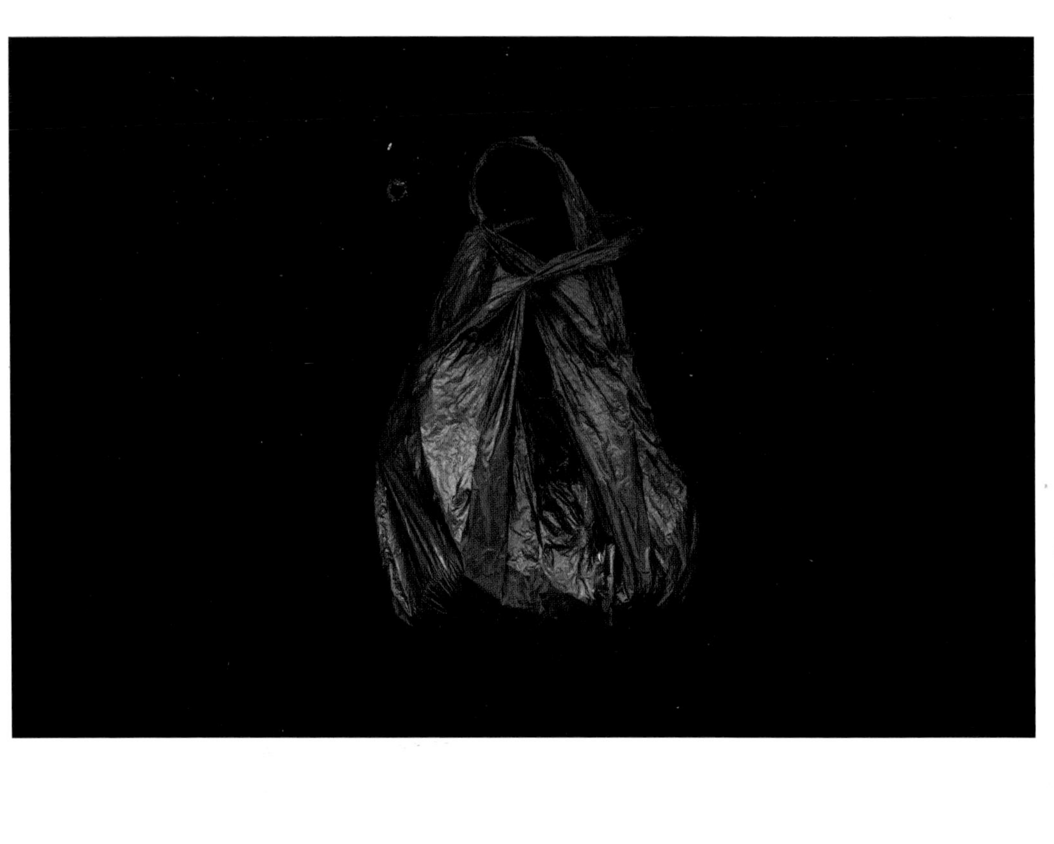